THE DRAGON

The Hebrews call it Thanin, and Wolphius translateth Oach a Dragon, in his Commentaries upon Nehemiah. The Chaldees call it Darkon, and it seemeth that the Greek word Dracon is derived of the Chaldee. We read of Albedisimon, or Abedysimon, for a kinde of Dragon, and also Alhatraf, and Hauden, Harencarnem, and such other terms. The Grecians at this day call it Drakos ; the Germans, Trach Lindtwarm ; the French, Un Dragon ; the Italians, Drago, and Dragone. The derivation of the Greek word, beside the conjecture afore expressed, some think to be derived from Derkein, because of their vigilant eye-sight, and therefore it is faigned that they had the custody not only of the Golden fleece, but also of many other treasures.

Edward Topsell,
THE HISTORY OF SERPENTS,
London, 1658

THE DRAGON

Charles Gould
and others

EDITED by MALCOLM SMITH

WILDWOOD HOUSE LONDON

First published 1977
Copyright © Unicorn Bookshop, 1977

Wildwood House Limited
29 King Street
London WC2E 8JD

ISBN 0 7045 0277 1

The extract from 'St. George'
by Sabine Baring-Gould is taken
from *Curious Myths of the
Middle Ages*, London 1869.

Printed and bound in Great Britain
by Biddles Ltd, Guildford, Surrey
and Henry Brooks Ltd, Oxford.

contents

Passages from Edward Topsell's ' The History of Serpents '
appear on pages : 2, 6, 8, 44, 62, 86, 98, and 104.

When the Region of Helvetia began first to be purged from noysome Beasts, there was a horrible Dragon found neer a Countrey Town called Wilser, who did destroy all men and beasts that came within his danger in the time of his hunger, insomuch that that Town and the fields thereto adjoyning, was called Dedwiler, that is, a Village of the Wildernesse, for all the people and Inhabitants had forsaken the same, and fled to other places.

There was a man of that Town whose name was Winckelriedt, who was banished for man-slaughter, this man promised if he might have his pardon, and be restored again to his former Inheritance, that he would combate with that Dragon, and by Gods help destroy him: which thing was granted unto him with great joyfulnesse. Wherefore he was recalled home, and in the presence of many people went forth to fight with the Dragon, whom he slew and overcame, whereat for joy he lifted up his sword imbrued in the Dragons bloud, in token of victory, but the bloud distilled down from his sword upon his body, and caused him instantly to fall down dead.

Edward Topsell,
THE HISTORY OF SERPENTS,
London, 1658.

The
WESTERN DRAGON

Gillius, Pierius, and Grevinus do affirm that a Dragon is of a black colour, the belly somewhat green, and very beautiful to behold, having a treble row of teeth in their mouths upon every jaw, and with most bright and cleer seeing eyes, which caused the Poets to faign in their writings, that these Dragons are the watchfull keepers of Treasures. They have also two dewlaps growing under their chin, and hanging down like a beard, which are of a red colour : their bodies are set all over with very sharp scales, and over their eyes stand certain flexible eyelids. When they gape wide with their mouth, and thrust forth their tongue, their teeth seem very much to resemble the teeth of wilde Swine. And their necks have many times grosse thick hair growing upon them, much like unto the bristles of a wilde Boar.

Edward Topsell,
THE HISTORY OF SERPENTS,
London, 1658.

THE DRAGON AND THE SERPENT

The dragon is defined in the Encyclopaedia Britannica for 1877 as "the name given by the ancients to a huge winged lizard or serpent (fabulous) ".

The text also goes on to state that "they (the ancients) regarded it as the enemy of mankind, and its overthrow is made to figure among the greatest exploits of the gods and heroes of heathen mythology. A dragon watched the gardens of the Hesperides, and its destruction formed one of the seven labours of Hercules. Its existence does not seem to have been called in question by the older naturalists ; figures of the dragon appearing in the works of Gesner and Aldrovandus, and even specimens of the monster, evidently formed artificially of portions of different animals, have been exhibited." A reference is also made to the genus Draco, comprising eighteen specimens of winged lizards, all small, and peculiar to India and the islands of the Malay archipelago.

Such is the meagre account of a creature which figures in the history and mythology of all nations, which in its different forms has been worshipped as a god, endowed with beneficent and malevolent attributes, combatted as a monster, or supposed to have possessed supernatural power, exercised alternately for the benefit or chastisement of mankind.

Its existence is inseparably wedded to the history, from the most remote antiquity, of a nation which possesses connected and authentic memoirs stretching uninterruptedly from the present day far into the remote past ; on which the belief in its existence has been so strongly impressed, that it retains its emblem in its insignia of office, in its ornamentation of furniture, utensils, and dwellings, and commemorates it annually in the competition of

dragon boats, and the processions of dragon images ; which believes, or
affects to believe, in its continued existence in the pools of the deep, and the
clouds of the sky ; which propitiates it with sacrifices and ceremonies, builds
temples in its honour, and cultivates its worship ; whose legends and traditions
teem with anecdotes of its interposition in the affairs of man, and whose
scientific works, of antiquity rivalling that of our oldest Western Classics,
treat of its existence as a sober and accepted fact, and differentiate its species
with some exactness. It is, moreover, though not very frequently, occasionally
referred to in the Biblical history of that other ancient, and almost equally
conservative branch of the human race, the Jews, not as a myth, or doubtfully
existent supernatural monster, but as a tangible reality, an exact terrible
creature.

Equally do we find it noticed in those other valuable records of the past
which throw cross lights upon the Bible narrative, and confirm by collateral
facts the value of its historic truth ; such as the fragments of Chaldean history
handed down by the reverent care of later historians, the careful narrative of
Josephus, and the grand resurrection of Chaldean and Assyrian lore effected
by the marvellously well directed and fortunate labour of G.H. Smith and those
who follow in his train.

Among the earliest classics of Europe, its existence is asserted as a
scientific fact, and accepted by poets as a sound basis for analogies, compar-
isons, allegories, and fable ; it appears in the mythology of the Goth, and is
continued through the tradition and fable of every country of Europe ; nor does
it fail to appear even in the imperfect traditions of the New World, where its
presence may be considered as comparatively indigenous, and undetermined
by the communications dependent on the so-called discovery of later days.

Turning to other popular accounts, we find equally limited and incredible versions of it. All consider it sufficiently disposed of by calling it
fabulous, and that a sufficient explanation of any possible belief in it is
afforded by a reference to the harmless genus of existing flying lizards
referred to above.

Some consider it an evolution of the fancy, typifying noxious principles ;
thus, Chambers says, "The dragon appears in the mythical history and
legendary poetry of almost every nation as the emblem of the destructive and
anarchical principle ; ... as misdirected physical force and untamable animal
passions ... The dragon proceeds openly to work, running on its feet with
expanded wings, and head and tail erect, violently and ruthlessly outraging
decency and propriety, spouting fire and fury both from mouth and tail, and
wasting and devastating the whole land."

10

The point which strikes me as most interesting in this passage is the reference to the legendary theory of the mode of the dragon's progress, which curiously calls to mind the semi-erect attitude of the existing small Australian frilled lizard (Chlamydosaurus). This attitude is also ascribed to some of the extinct American Dinosaurs, such as the Stegosaurus.

No one, so far as I am aware, in late days has hitherto ventured to up-uphold the claims of this terrible monster to be accepted as a real contempo-rary of primitive man, which may even have been co-existent with him to a comparatively recent date, and but lately passed away into the cohort of extinct species, leaving behind it only the traditions of its ferocity and terrors, to stamp their impression on the tongues of all countries.

No one has endeavoured to collate the vast bulk of materials shrouded in the stories of all lands. If this were perfectly effected, a diagnosis of the real nature of the dragon might perhaps be made, and the chapter of its characteristics, alliances, and habits completed like that of any other well-established species.

The following sketch purposes only to initiate the task here propounded, the author's access to materials being limited, and only sufficient to enable him, as he thinks, to establish generally the proposition which it involves, to grasp as it were some of the broader and salient features of the investigation, while leaving a rich gleaning of corroborative information for the hand of any other who may please to continue and extend his observations.

At the outset it will be necessary to assign a much more extended signification to the word dragon than that which is contained in the definition at the head of this chapter. The popular mind of the present day doubtless associates it always with the idea of a creature possessing wings ; but the Lung of the Chinese, the δρακων of the Greeks, the Draco of the Romans, the Egyptian dragon, and the Naga of the Sanscrit have no such limited signification, and appear to have been sometimes applied to any serpent, lacertian, or saurian, of extraordinary dimensions, nor is it always easy to determine from the passages in which these several terms occur what kind of monster is specially indicated.

Thus the dragon referred to by Propertius in the quotation annexed may have been a large python. "Lanuvium is, of old, protected by an aged dragon ; here, where the occasion of an amusement so seldom occurring is not lost, where is the abrupt descent into a dark and hollowed cave ; where is let down — maiden, beware of every such journey — the honorary tribute to the fast-ing snake, when he demands his yearly food, and hisses and twists deep down in the earth. Maidens, let down for such a rite, grow pale, when their hand is unprotectedly trusted in the snake's mouth. He snatches at the delicacies if offered by a maid ; the very baskets tremble in the virgin's hands ; if they are chaste, they return and fall on the necks of their parents, and the farmers cry 'We shall have a fruitful year '." (1)

To the same class may probably be ascribed the dragon referred to by Aristotle (2). "The eagle and the dragon are enemies, for the eagle feeds on serpents " ; and again (3), "the Glanis in shallow water is often destroyed by the dragon serpent". It might perhaps be supposed that the crocodile is here referred to, but this is specially spoken of in another passage, as follows (4) : "But there are others which, though they live and feed in the water, do not take in water but air, and produce their young out of the water ; many of these animals are furnished with feet, as the otter and crocodile, and others are without feet, as the water-serpent".

A somewhat inexplicable habit is ascribed to the dragon in Book ix (5) : "When the draco has eaten much fruit, it seeks the juice of the bitter lettuce ; it has been seen to do this ".

Pliny, probably quoting Aristotle, also states that the dragon relieves the nausea which affects it in spring with the juices of the lettuce ; and Ælian repeats the story.

It is also probable that some large serpent is intended by Pliny in the story which he relates (6), after Democritus, that a man called Thoas was preserved in Arcadia by a dragon. When a boy, he had become attached to it and had reared it very tenderly ; but his father, being alarmed at the nature and monstrous size of the reptile, had taken and left it in the desert. Thoas being here attacked by robbers who lay in ambush, he was delivered from them by the dragon, which recognized his voice and came to his assistance. It may be noted in regard to this that there are many authenticated instances of snakes evidencing considerable affection for those who have treated them with kindness.

The impression that Pliny's dragon was intended to represent some large boa or python is strengthened by his statement (7) : "The dragon is a serpent destitute of venom ; its head placed beneath the threshold of a door, the gods being duly propitiated by prayers, will ensure good fortune to the house, it is said".

It is remarkable that he attributes to the dragon the same desire and capacity to attack the elephant as is attributed to the Pa snake in Western

12

China, and by the old Arabian voyagers to serpents in Borneo.

The Shan-hai-king, a Chinese work of extreme antiquity, of which special mention will be made hereafter, says : "The Pa snake swallows elephants, after three years it ejects the bones ; well-to-do people, eating it, are cured of consumption".

Diodorus Siculus, in speaking of the region of the Nile in Libya, says that, according to report, very large serpents are produced there and in great numbers, and that these attack elephants when they gather around the watering places, involve them in their folds till they fall exhausted, and then devour them.

Diodorus, in another passage referring to the crocodiles and hippopotami of Egypt, speaking of Ethiopia and Libya, mentions a variety of serpents as well as of other wild beasts, including dragons of unusual size and ferocity.

While El Edrisi says : "One might also mention the serpent of Zaledj spoken of by Ben Khordadébe, the author of The Book of Marvels and several other writings which agree in saying that there exists, in the mountains of the island of Zaledj, a species of serpent which attacks the elephant and buffalo, and which will not release them until after they are overcome". (8)

Artemidorus, also, according to Strabo (9), "mentions serpents of thirty cubits in length, which can master elephants and bulls. In this he does not exaggerate ; but the Indian and African serpents are of a more fabulous size, and are said to have grass growing on their backs ".

Iphicrates, according to Bryant, "related that in Mauritania there were dragons of such extent that grass grew upon their backs ".

It is doubtful whether large serpents, or real dragons, are referred to by Pliny in the following interesting passages which I give at length : the surprise which he expresses at Juba's believing that they had crests, leads me to suspect that there was possibly some confusion of species involved ; that Juba might have been perfectly accurate so far as the crests are concerned, and that the beasts in question, in place of being pythons of magnitude, were rather some gigantic lizard-like creature, of great length and little bulk, corresponding with the Chinese idea of the dragon, and, therefore, naturally bearing horny crests, similar to those with which the monster is usually represented by the latter people.

It must be noticed here, that if we postulate the existence of the dragon,

13

we are not bound to limit ourselves to a single species, or even two, as the same causes which effected the gradual destruction of one would be exceedingly likely to effect that of another ; we must not, therefore, be too critical in comparing descriptions of different authors in different countries and epochs, since they may refer only to allied, but not identical, animals.

"Africa produces elephants, but it is India that produces the largest, as well as the dragon, who is perpetually at war with the elephant, and is itself of so enormous a size, as easily to envelop the elephants with its folds, and encircle them in its coils. The contest is equally fatal to both ; the elephant, vanquished, falls to the earth, and by its weight crushes the dragon which is entwined around it.   (10)

"The sagacity which every animal exhibits in its own behalf is wonderful, but in these it is remarkably so. The dragon has much difficulty in climbing up to so great a height, and therefore, watching the road, which bears marks of their footsteps, when going to feed, it darts down upon them from a lofty tree. The elephant knows that it is quite unable to struggle against the folds of the serpent, and so seeks for trees or rocks against which to rub itself.

"The dragon is on its guard against this, and tries to prevent it, by first of all confining the legs of the elephant with the folds of its tail ; while the elephant, on the other hand, tries to disengage itself with its trunk. The dragon, however, thrusts its head into its nostrils, and thus, at the same moment, stops the breath and wounds the most tender parts. When it is met unexpectedly, the dragon raises itself up, faces its opponent, and flies more especially at the eyes ; this is the reason why elephants are so often found blind, and worn to a skeleton with hunger and misery.

"There is another story, too, told in relation to these combats. The blood of the elephant, it is said, is remarkably cold ; for which reason, in the parching heats of summer, it is sought by the dragon with remarkable avidity. It lies, therefore, coiled up and concealed in the river, in wait for the elephants when they come to drink ; upon which it darts out, fastens itself around the trunk, and then fixes its teeth behind the ear, that being the only place which the elephant cannot protect with the trunk. The dragons, it is said, are of such vast size that they can swallow the whole of the blood ; consequently the elephant, being drained of its blood, falls to the earth exhausted ; while the dragon, intoxicated with the draught, is crushed beneath it, and so shares its fate.   (11)

"Ethiopia produces dragons, not so large as those of India, but still twenty cubits in length. The only thing that surprises me is, how Juba came to

14

believe that they have crests. The Ethiopians are known as the Asachaei, among whom they most abound ; and we are told that on those coasts four or five of them are found twisted and interlaced together like so many osiers in a hurdle, and thus setting sail, with their heads erect, they are borne along upon the waves to find better sources of nourishment in Arabia (12)."

Pliny then goes on to describe, as separate from dragons, large serpents in India, as follows.

"Megasthenes (13) informs us that in India serpents grow to such an immense size as to swallow stags and bulls ; while Metrodorus says that about the river Rhyndacus, in Pontus, they seize and swallow the birds that are flying above them, however high and however rapid their flight.

"It is a well-known fact that during the Punic war, at the river Bagrada, a serpent one hundred and twenty feet in length was taken by the Roman army under Regulus, being beseiged, like a fortress, by means of balistae and other engines of war. Its skin and jaws were preserved in a temple at Rome down to the time of the Numantine war.

"The serpents, which in Italy are known by the name of boa, render these accounts far from incredible, for they grow to such vast size that a child was found entire in the stomach of one of them which was killed on the Vaticanian Hill during the reign of Emperor Claudius."

Aristotle tells us that "in Libya, the serpents, as it has been already remarked, are very large. For some persons say that as they sailed along the coast, they saw the bones of many oxen, and that it was evident to them that they had been devoured by serpents. And, as the ships passed on, the serpents attacked the triremes, and some of them threw themselves upon one of the triremes and overturned it." (14)

It is doubtful whether the dragons described by Benjamin of Tudela, who travelled through Europe and the East and returned to Castille in 1173, as infesting the ruins of the palace of Nebuchodonosor at Babylon, so as to render them inaccessible, were creatures of the imagination such as the medieval mind seems to have loved to dress up, or venomous serpents. But there is little doubt that the so-called dragons of later voyages were simply boas, pythons, or other large serpents, such as those described by John Leo, in his description of a voyage to Africa, as existing in the caverns of Atlas. He says, "There are many monstrous dragons which are thick about the middle, but have slender necks and tails, so that their motion is but slow. They are so venomous, that whatever they bite or touch, certain death ensues (15)".

15

There is also the statement of Job Ludolphus that (in Ethiopia) "the dragons are of the largest size, very voracious, but not venomous". (16)

I fancy that at the present day the numbers, magnitude, and terrifying nature of serpents but feebly represent the power which they asserted in the early days of man's existence, or the terror which they then inspired. This subject has been so ably dealt with by a writer of the last century (17) that I feel no hesitation in transcribing his remarks at length.

"It is probable, in early times, when the arts were little known and mankind were but thinly scattered over the earth, that serpents, continuing undisturbed possessors of the forest, grew to an amazing magnitude, and every other tribe of animals fell before them. It then might have happened that the serpents reigned tyrants of the district for centuries together. To animals of this kind, grown by time and rapacity to one hundred or one hundred and fifty feet long, the lion, the tiger, and even the elephant itself were but feeble opponents. That horrible fetor, which even the commonest and the most harmless snakes are still found to diffuse, might in these larger ones become too powerful for any living being to withstand, and while they preyed without distinction, they might also have poisoned the atmosphere round them. In this manner, having for ages lived in the hidden and unpeopled forest, and finding, as their appetites were more powerful, the quantity of their prey decreasing, it is possible they might venture boldly from their retreats into the more cultivated parts of the country, and carry consternation among mankind, as they had before desolation among the lower ranks of nature.

"We have many histories of antiquity presenting us such a picture, and exhibiting a whole nation sinking under the ravages of a single serpent. At that time man had not learned the art of uniting the efforts of many to effect one great purpose. Opposing multitudes only added new victims to the general calamity, and increased mutual embarrassment and terror. The animal, therefore, was to be singly opposed by him who had the greatest strength, the best armour, and the most undaunted courage. In such an encounter hundreds must have fallen, till one more lucky than the rest, by a fortunate blow, or by taking the monster in its torpid interval and surcharged with spoil, might kill and thus rid his country of the destroyer. Such was the original occupation of heroes.

"But as we descend into more enlightened antiquity we find these animals less formidable, as being attacked in a more successful manner.

"We are told that while Regulus led his army along the banks of the river Bagrada in Africa, an enormous serpent disputed his passage over. We

16

are assured by Pliny that it was one hundred and twenty feet long, and that it had destroyed many of the army. At last, however, the battering engines were brought out against it, and then, assailing it at a distance, it was destroyed. Its spoils were carried to Rome, and the general was decreed an ovation for his success.

"There are, perhaps, few facts better ascertained in history than this : an ovation was a remarkable honour, and was only given for some signal exploit that did not deserve a triumph. No historian would offer to invent that part of the story, at least, without being subject to the most shameful detection.

"The skin was kept for several years after, in the Capitol, and Pliny says he saw it there.

"This tribe of animals, like that of fishes, seem to have no bounds put to their growth ; their bones are in a great measure cartilaginous, and they are consequently capable of great extension.

"The older, therefore, a serpent becomes, the larger it grows, and, as they live to a great age, they arrive at an enormous size. Leguat assures us that he saw one in Java that was fifty feet long (18). Carli mentions their growing to above forty feet, and there is now in the British Museum one that measures thirty-two feet.

"Mr. Wentworth, who had large concerns in the Berbice in America, assures us that in that country they grow to an enormous length. He describes an Indian mistaking one for a log, and proceeding to sit down on it, when it began to move. A soldier with him shot the snake, but the Indian died of fright. It measured thirty-six feet. It was sent to the Hague.

"A life of savage hostility in the forest offers the imagination one of the most tremendous pictures in nature. In those burning countries where the sun dries up every brook for hundreds of miles around : where what had the appearance of a great river in the rainy season becomes in summer one dreary bed of sand ; in those countries a lake that is never dry, or a brook that is perennial, is considered by every animal as the greatest convenience of nature. When they have discovered this, no dangers can deter them from attempting to slake their thirst. Thus the neighbourhood of a rivulet, in the heart of the tropical continents, is generally the place where all the hostile tribes of nature draw up for the engagement.

"On the banks of this little envied spot, thousands of animals of various kinds are seen venturing to quench their thirst, or preparing to seize their prey. The elephants are perceived in a long line, marching from the darker parts of the forest. The buffaloes are there, depending upon numbers for security ; the gazelles relying solely upon their swiftness ; the lion and tiger waiting a proper opportunity to seize.

"But chiefly the larger serpents are upon guard there, and defend the accesses of the lake. Not an hour passes without some dreadful combat, but the serpent, defended by its scales, and naturally capable of sustaining a multitude of wounds, is of all others the most formidable. It is the most wakeful also, for the whole tribe sleep with their eyes open, and are consequently for ever upon the watch ; so that, till their rapacity is satisfied, few other animals will venture to approach their station".

We read of a serpent exhibited in the time of Augustus at Rome, which, Seutonius tells us, "was fifty cubits in length" (19). But at the present day there are few authentic accounts of snakes exceeding thirty feet in length ; and there are some people who discredit any which profess to speak of snakes of greater dimensions than this. There are some, however, among the annexed stories, which I think demand belief, and apparently we may conclude that the python and boa exceptionally attain as much as forty feet in length, or even more.

Wallace (20) merely reports by hearsay that the pythons in the Phillipines , which destroy young cattle, are said to reach more than forty feet.

Captain Sherard Osborn (21), in his description of Quedah in the Malay peninsula, says, also, as a matter of popular belief : "The natives of Tamelan declared most of them to be of the boa-constrictor species, but spoke of monsters in the deep forests, which might, if they came out, clear off the whole village. A pleasant feat, for which Jadie, with a wag of his sagacious head, assured me that an ' oular Bessar ' or big snake was quite competent.

"It was strange but interesting to find amongst all Malays a strong belief in the extraordinary size to which the boa-constrictors or pythons would grow ; they all maintained that in the secluded forests of Sumatra or Borneo, as well as on some of the smaller islands which were not inhabited, these snakes were occasionally found of forty or fifty feet in length".

Major McNair says (22): "One of the keenest sportsmen in Singapore gives an account of a monster that he encountered. He had wounded a boar in the jungle, and was following its tracks with his dogs, when, in penetrating

The Medieval Dragon (above) shown with some of the creatures that leant substance and credibility to its legend. <u>Left</u>: The Indian Python.　<u>Below</u>: The Gavial and Nile Crocodile. Bottom :: The Dinosaur, which, in this early reconstruction, clearly derives in turn from the traditional image of the dragon.

The winged dragon engraved by Lucas Cranach (top right), with its boar's head and beetle's wings, is matched in Nature by the flying lizards of the genus Draco (above), found in India and the Malay Archipelago. No less strange than the heavily armoured dragor of legend is the small Australian lizard, Moloch Horridus (right), protected the entire length of its body by a fearsome array of thorny spikes.

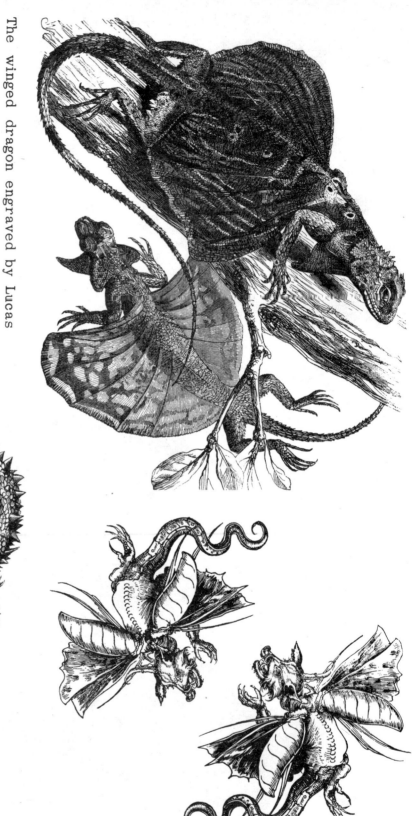

PLATE TWO

further into the forest, he found the dogs at bay, and, advancing cautiously, prepared for another shot at the boar ; to his surprise, however, he found that the dogs were baying at a huge python, which had seized the boar, thrown its coils round the unfortunate beast, and was crushing it to death. A well-directed shot laid the reptile writhing on the ground, and it proved to be about thirty feet long. But such instances of extreme length are rare ".

Unfortunately the exciting story of a serpent, between forty and fifty feet in length, which I extract from the North China Daily News of November 10th, 1880, the scene of which is also laid in the Malay peninsula, lacks the authenticity of the narrator's name. It is as follows : —

"The Straits Times tells the following exciting python story : ' A sportsman, who a few days ago penetrated into the jungle lying between Buddoh and Sirangoon, came upon a lone hut in a district called Campong Batta, upon the roof of which the skin of an enormous boa or python (whichever may be the correct name) was spread out. The hut was occupied by a Malay and his wife, from whom our informant gathered the following extraordinary account. One night, about a week previously, the Malay was awakened by the cries of his wife for assistance. Being in perfect darkness, and supposing the alarm to be on account of thieves, he seized his sharp parang, and groped his way to her sleeping place, where his hand fell upon a slimy reptile. It was fully a minute before he could comprehend the entire situation, and when he did, he discovered that the whole of his wife's arm had been drawn down the monster's throat, whither the upper part of her body was slowly but surely following. Not daring to attack the monster at once for fear of causing his wife's death, the husband, with great presence of mind, seized two bags within reach, and commenced stuffing them into the corner of the snake's jaws, by means of which he succeeded in forcing them wider open and releasing his wife's arm. No sooner had the boa lost his prey than he attacked the husband, whom he began encircling in his fatal coils ; but holding out both arms, and watching his opportunity, he attacked the monster so vigorously with his parang that it suddenly unwound itself and vanished through an opening beneath the attap sides of the hut. His clothes were covered with blood, as was also the floor of the hut, and his wife's arm was blue with the squeezing it received between the boa's jaws. At daylight the husband discovered his patch of plantain trees nearly ruined, where the boa, writhing in agony, had broken off the trees at the roots, and in the midst of the debris lay the monster itself, dead. The Malay assured our informant that he had received no less than sixty dollars from Chinese, who came from long distances to purchase pieces of the flesh on account of its supposed medical properties, and that he had refused six dollars for the skin, which he preferred to retain as a trophy. It was greatly decomposed, having been some days exposed in the open air, and useless for curing. There is no telling what may have been the measurement of this large reptile, but the skin, probably greatly stretched by unskilful removal, measured between seven and eight fathoms".

Bontius speaks of serpents in the Asiatic Isles. "The great ones," he says, "sometimes exceed thirty-six feet ; and have such capacity of throat and stomach that they swallow whole boars."

Mr. McLeod, in the 'Voyage of the Alceste', states that during a captivity of some months at Whidah, on the coast of Africa, he had opportunities of observing serpents double this length. (23)

Broderip, in his 'Leaves from the Note-book of a Naturalist' (Parker, 1852), speaks of a serpent thirty feet in length, which attacked the crew of a Malay proa anchored for the night close to the island of Celebes.

Mr. C. Collingwood, in 'Rambles of a Naturalist', states that "Mr. Low assured me that he had seen one (python) killed measuring twenty-six feet, and I heard on good authority of one of twenty-nine feet having been killed there. In Borneo they were said to attain forty feet, but for this I cannot vouch."

That large pythons still exist in South and Western China, although of very reduced dimensions as compared with those described in ancient works, is affirmed by many writers, from whom I think it is sufficient to extract a notice by one of the early missionaries who explored that country.

"Pour ce qui est des serpens qu'on trouve dans Chine l'Atlas raconte que la Province de Quansi, en produit de si grands et d'une longueur si extrême, qu'il est presque incroyable ; et il nous assure, qu'il s'en est trouvé, qui étaient plus longs que ne seraient pas dix perches attachées les unes avec les autres, c'est-à-dire, qu'ils avaient plus de trente pieds géométriques. Flore Sienois dit, ' Gento est le plus grand de tous ceux qui sont dans les provinces de Quansi, de Haynan, et de Quantun ... il dévore les cerfs ... Il s'élève droit sur sa queue, et combat vigoureusement, en cette posture, contre les hommes et les bêtes farouches'." (24)

We have unfortunately no clue to the actual length of the serpent Bomma, described by J.M. da Sorrento in 'A Voyage to Congo' in 1682, contained in Churchill's collection of voyages published in 1732 (25). "The flesh they eat is generally that of wild creatures, and especially of a sort of serpent called Bomma. At a certain feast in Baia, I observed the windows, instead of tapestry and arras, adorned with the skin of these serpents as wide as that of a large ox, and long in proportion."

That harmless snakes of from twelve to fourteen feet in length occur abundantly in Northern Australia is generally known ; but it is only of late years that I have been made acquainted with a firm belief, entertained by the natives in the interior, of the existence near the junction of the Darling and Murray, south of the centre of the continent, of a serpent of great magnitude.

I learn from Mr. G.R. Moffat that on the Lower Murray, between Swan Hill and the Darling junction — at the time of his acquaintance with the district (about 1857 to 1867) — the black fellows had numerous stories of the existence of a large serpent in the Mallee scrub. It was conspicuous for its size, thirty to forty feet in length, and especially for its great girth, swiftness, and intensely disgusting odour ; this latter, in fact, constituted the great protection from it, insomuch as it would be impossible to approach without recognising its presence.

Mr. Moffat learnt personally from a Mr. Beveridge, son of Mr. Peter Beveridge, of Swan Hill station, that he had actually seen one, and that his account quite tallied with those of the blacks. In answer to an inquiry which I addressed to Australia, I received the note attached below : —

"With reference to the Mindi or Mallee snake, it has often been described to me as a formidable creature of at least thirty feet in length, which confined itself to the Mallee scrub. No one, however, has ever seen one, for the simple reason that to see it is to die, so fierce it is, and so great its power of destruction. Like the Bunyip, I believe the Mindi to be a myth, a mere tradition " — Mr. C.M. Officer, Proceedings of the Royal Society of Tasmania, September 13th, 1880.

Mr. Henry Liddell, who was resident on the Darling River in 1871-72, informs me that he has heard from stock-riders and ration-carriers similar accounts to that of Mr. Moffat, with reference to the existence of large serpents of the boa species in an adjacent locality, viz. the tract of country lying to the east of Darling and Murray junction, in the back country belonging to Pooncaira station.

They described them as being numerous, in barren and rocky places, among big boulders ; fully forty feet long ; as thick as a man's thigh ; and as having the same remarkable odour described by Mr. Moffat. They spoke of them as quite common, and not at all phenomenal, between Wentworth and Pooncaira.

The Anaconda, in regard to which so much myth and superstition prevails among the Indians of Brazil, is thus spoken of by Condamine, in his

'Travels in South America'. "The most rare and singular of all is a large amphibious serpent from twenty-five to thirty feet long and more than a foot thick, according to report. It is called Jacumama, or 'the mother of the waters', by the Americans of Maynas, and commonly inhabits the large lakes formed by the river-water after flood." (26)

Ulloa, also, in his 'Voyage to South America', says : "In the countries watered by that vast river (the Maranon) is bred a serpent of a frightful magnitude, and of a most deleterious nature. Some, in order to give an idea of its largeness, affirm that it will swallow any beast whole, and that this has been the miserable end of many a man. But what seems still a greater wonder is the attractive quality attributed to its breath, which irresistibly draws any creature to it which happens to be within the sphere of its attraction. The Indians call it Jacumama, i.e. 'mother of water' ; for, as it delights in lakes and marshy places, it may in some sense be considered as amphibious. I have taken a great deal of pains to inquire into this particular, and all I can say is that the reptile's magnitude is really surprising." (27)

John Nieuhoff, in his 'Voyage to Brazil', speaking of the serpent Guaku or Liboya, says : "It is questionless the biggest of all serpents, some being eighteen, twenty-four, nay thirty feet long, and of the thickness of a man in his middle. The Portuguese call it Kobra Detrado, or the roebuck serpent, because it will swallow a whole roebuck, or any other deer it meets with ; after they have swallowed such a deer, they fall asleep, and so are catched. Such a one I saw at Paraiba, which was thirty feet long, and as big as a barrel. This serpent, being a very devouring creature, greedy of prey, leaps from amongst the hedges and woods, and standing upright upon its tail, wrestles both with men and wild beasts ; sometimes it leaps from the trees upon the traveller, whom it fastens upon, and beats the breath out of his body with its tail." (28)

The largest (water boa) ever met with by a European appears to be that described by a botanist, Dr. Gardiner, in his 'Travels in Brazil'. It had devoured a horse, and was found dead, entangled in the branches of a tree overhanging a river, into which it had been carried by a flood ; it was nearly forty feet long.

WINGED SERPENTS

The next section relates to winged serpents, a belief in which was prevalent in early ages, and is strongly supported by several independent works.

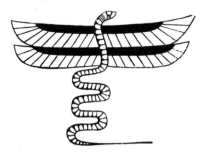

Egyptian
Winged Serpents

To my mind, Herodotus speaks without the slightest doubt upon the subject in the following passages. "Arabia is the last of inhabited lands towards the south, and it is the only country which produces frankincense, myrrh, cassia, cinnamon, and ledanum." "The frankincense they procure by means of the gum styrax, which the Greeks get from the Phoenicians. This they burn, and thereby obtain the spice ; for the trees which bear the frankincense are guarded by winged serpents, small in size, and of various colours, whereof vast numbers hang about every tree. They are of the same kind as the serpents that invade Egypt, and there is nothing but the smoke of the styrax which will drive them from the trees." (29)

Again, "the Arabians say that the whole world would swarm with these serpents, if they were not kept in check, in the way which I know that vipers are." "Now, with respect to the vipers and the winged snakes of Arabia, if they increased as fast as their nature would allow, impossible were it for man to maintain himself upon the earth. Accordingly, it is found that when the male and female come together, at the very moment of impregnation, the female seizes the male by the neck, and having once fastened cannot be brought to leave go till she has bit the neck entirely through, and so the male perishes ; but after a while he is avenged upon the female by means of the young, which, while still unborn, gnaw a passage through the womb and then through the belly of their mother. Contrariwise, other snakes, which are harmless, lay eggs and hatch a vast number of young. Vipers are found in all parts of the world, but the winged serpents are nowhere seen except in Arabia, where they are all congregated together ; this makes them appear so numerous." (30)

Herodotus had so far interested himself in ascertaining the probability of their existence as to visit Arabia for the purpose of inquiry ; he says (31),

25

"I went once to a certain place in Arabia, almost exactly opposite the city of Buto, to make inquiries concerning the winged serpents. On my arrival I saw the back-bones and ribs of serpents in such numbers as it is impossible to describe; of the ribs there were a multitude of heaps, some great, some small, some middle-sized. The place where the bones lie is at the entrance of a narrow gorge between steep mountains, which there open upon a spacious plain communicating with the great plains of Egypt. The story goes, that with the spring the snakes come flying from Arabia towards Egypt, but are met in this gorge by the birds called ibises, who forbid their entrance and destroy them all. The Arabians assert, and the Egyptians also admit, that it is on account of the service thus rendered that the Egyptians hold the ibis in so much reverence." He further describes the winged serpent as being shaped like the water-snake, and states that its wings are not feathered, but resemble very closely those of the bat.

Winged Serpents : Western (above) and Chinese (below).

Aristotle briefly states, as a matter of common report, that there were in his time winged serpents in Ethiopia (32). Both two and four winged snakes are depicted among the Egyptian sculptures, considered by Mr. Cooper to be emblematic of deities, and to signify that the four corners of the earth are embraced and sheltered by the supreme Providence.

Josephus (33) unmistakably affirms his belief in the existence of flying serpents, in his account of the stratagem which Moses adopted in attacking the Ethiopians, who had invaded Egypt and penetrated as far as Memphis. From this we may infer that in his time flying serpents were by no means peculiar to Arabia, but, as might have been expected, equally infested the desert lands bordering the fertile strip of the Nile.

In Whiston's translation we read that "Moses prevented the enemies, and took and led his army before those enemies were apprised of his attacking them ; for he did not march by the river, but by land, where he gave a wonderful demonstration of his sagacity ; for when the ground was difficult to be passed over, because of the multitude of serpents (which it produces in vast numbers, and indeed is singular in some of these productions, which other countries do not breed, and yet such as are worse than others in power and mischief, and an unusual fierceness of sight, some of which ascend out of the ground unseen, and also fly in the air, and so come upon men at unawares, and do them a mischief), Moses invented a wonderful stratagem to preserve the army safe and without hurt; for he made baskets, like unto arks, of sedge, and filled them with ibes, and carried them along with them; which animal is the greatest enemy to serpents imaginable, for they fly from them when they come near them; and as they fly they are caught and devoured by them, as if it were done by the harts; but the ibes are tame creatures, and only enemies to the serpentine kind; but about these ibes I say no more at present, since the Greeks themselves are not unacquainted with this sort of bird. As soon, therefore, as Moses was come to the land which was the breeder of these serpents, he let loose the ibes, and by their means repelled the serpentine kind, and used them for his assistants before the army came upon that ground."

These statements of Herodotus and Josephus are both too precise to be explicable on the theory that they refer to the darting or jumping serpents which Nieuhoff describes, in his day, as infesting the palm trees of Arabia and springing from tree to tree; or to the jaculus of Pliny (34), which darts from the branches of trees, and flies through the air as though it were hurled by an engine, and which is described by Ælian and graphically figured by Lucan (35) in the passage — "Behold! afar, around the trunk of a barren tree, a fierce serpent — Africa calls it the jaculus — wreathes itself, and then darts forth, and through the head and pierced temples of Paulus it takes its flight: nothing does venom there effect, death seizes him through the wound. It was then understood how slowly fly the stones which the sling hurls, how sluggishly whizzes the flight of the Scythian arrow."

Solinus, whose work 'Polyhistor' is mainly a compilation from Pliny's Natural History, gives a similar account of the swarms of winged serpents about the Arabian marshes, and states that their bite was so deadly that death followed the bite before pain could be felt; he also refers to their destruction by the ibises, and is probably only quoting other authors rather than speaking of his own knowledge.

Cicero, again, speaks of the ibis as being a very large bird, with strong legs, and a horny long beak, which destroys a great number of serpents, and keeps Egypt free from pestilential diseases, by killing and devouring the flying serpents, brought from the deserts of Lybia by the south-west wind, and so preventing the mischief which might attend their biting while alive, or from any infection when dead.

There are not unfrequent allusions in ancient history to serpents having become so numerous as to constitute a perfect plague; the dreadful mortality caused among the Israelites by the fiery serpents spoken of in Numbers is a case in point, and another (36) is the migration of the Neuri from their own country into that of the Budini, one generation before the attack of Darius, in consequence of the incursion of a huge multitude of serpents. It is stated that some of these were produced in their own country, but for the most part they came in from the deserts of the north. The home of the Neuri appears to have been to the north-west of the Pontus Euxinus, pretty much in the position of Poland, and I believe that at the present day the only harmful reptile occurring in it is the viper common to the rest of Europe. Diodorus Siculus (37) mentions a tradition that the Cerastes had once made an irruption into Egypt in such numbers as to have depopulated a great portion of the inhabited districts.

These stories are interesting as showing a migratory instinct occurring in certain serpents, either periodically or occasionally, and are thus to some extent corroborative of the account of the annual invasion of Egypt by serpents, referred to in a previous page. They also, I think, confirm the impression that serpents were more numerous in the days of early history, and had a larger area of distribution than they have now, and that possibly some species, such as the Arabian and flying serpents, which have since become extinct, then existed. Thus the boa is spoken of by Pliny as occurring commonly in Italy, and growing to such a vast size that a child was found entire in one of them, which was killed on the Vatican Hill during the reign of the Emperor Claudius. Yet at the present day there are no snakes existing there at all corresponding to this description.

Parallel instances of invasions of animals materially affecting the prosperity of man are doubtless familiar to my readers, such as the occasional migration of lemmings, passage of rats, flights of locusts, or the ravages caused by the Colorado beetle ; but many are perhaps quite unaware what a terrible plague can be established, in the course of a very few years, by the prolific unchecked multiplication of even so harmless, innocent and useful an animal as the common rabbit. The descendants of a few imported pairs have laid waste extensive districts of Australia and New Zealand, necessitated an enormous expenditure for their extirpation, and have at the present day caused such a widespread destruction of property in the latter country, that large areas of ground have actually had to be abandoned and entirely surrendered to them.

It is interesting to find in the work of the Arabic geographer El Edrisi a tradition of an island in the Atlantic, called Laca, off the north-west coast of Africa, having been formerly inhabited, but abandoned on account of the excessive multiplication of serpents on it. According to Scaligerus, the mountains dividing the kingdom of Narsinga from Malabar produce many wild beasts, among which may be enumerated winged dragons, who are able to destroy anyone approaching their breath.

Megasthenes (tradente Æliano) relates that winged serpents are found in India ; where it is stated that they are noxious, fly only by night, and that contact with their urine destroys portions of animals.

Ammianus Marcellinus (who wrote about the fourth century A.D.) states that the ibis is one among the countless varieties of the birds of Egypt, sacred, amiable, and valuable as storing up the eggs of serpents in his nest for food and so diminishing their number. He also refers to their encountering flocks of winged snakes, coming laden with poison from the marshes of Arabia, and overcoming them in the air, and devouring them before they quit their own region. And Strabo (38), in his geographical description of India, speaks of serpents of two cubits in length, with membraneous wings like bats : "They fly at night, and let fall drops of urine or sweat, which occasions the skins of persons who are not on their guard to putrefy." Isaiah speaks of fiery flying serpents, the term "fiery" being otherwise rendered in the Alexandrine edition of the Septuagint by $\theta \alpha \nu \alpha \tau o \upsilon \nu \tau \epsilon \varsigma$ "deadly", while the term "fiery" is explained by other authorities as referring to the burning sensation produced by the bite, and to the bright colour of the serpents. Collateral evidence of the belief in winged serpents is afforded by incidental allusions to them in the classics. Thus Virgil alludes to snakes with strident wings in the line
Illa autem attolit stridentis anguibus alis (39).

Lucan (40) refers to the winged serpents of Arabia as forming one of the ingredients of an incantation broth brewed by a Thessalian witch, Erictho, with the object of resuscitating a corpse, and procuring replies to the queries of Sextus, son of Pompey. There are other passages in Ovid and other poets, in which the words "winged serpents" are made use of, but which I omit to render here, since from the context it seems doubtful whether they were not intended as poetic appellations of the monster to which, by popular consent, the term dragon has been generally restricted.

I feel bound to refer, although of course without attaching any very great weight of evidence to them, to the numerous stories popular in the East, in which flying serpents play a conspicuous part, the serpents always having something magical or supernatural in their nature. Such tales are found in the entrancing pages of the 'Arabian Nights', or in the very entertaining folk-lore of China.

The latest notice of the flying serpent that we find is in a work by P. Belon du Mans, published in 1557, entitled 'Portraits de quelques animaux, poissons, serpents, herbes et arbres, hommes et femmes d'Arabie, Egypte, et Asie, observés par P. Belon du Mans'. It contains a drawing of a biped winged dragon, with the notice "Portrait du serpent ailé " and the quatrain —

> Dangereuse est du serpent la nature
> Qu'on voit voler près le mont Sinai
> Qui ne serait, de la voir, esbahy,
> Si on a peur, voyant sa pourtraiture ?

This is copied by Gesner, who repeats the story of its flying out of Arabia into Egypt. I attach considerable importance to the short extract which I shall give in a future page from the celebrated Chinese work on geography and natural history, the Shan Hai King, or 'Mountain and Sea Classic'. The Shan Hai King claims to be of great antiquity, and, though long looked on with distrust, has been investigated recently by scholars of great ability, who have come to the conclusion that it is at least as old as the Chow dynasty, and probably older. Now, as the Chow dynasty commenced in 1122 B.C., it is, if this latter supposition be correct, of a prior age to the works of Aristotle, Herodotus, and all the other authors we have been quoting, and therefore is the earliest work on natural history extant, and the description of the flying serpent of the Sien mountains (vide infra) the earliest record of the existence of such creatures.

CLASSICAL AND MEDIEVAL DRAGONS

While the flying serpents of which we have just treated, will, if we assent to the reality of their former existence, assist greatly in the explanation of the belief in a winged dragon so far as Egypt, Arabia, and adjacent countries are concerned, it seems hardly probable that they are sufficient to account for the wide-spread belief in it. This we have already glanced at ; but we now propose to examine it in greater detail, with reference to countries so distant from their habitat as to render it unlikely that their description had penetrated there.

The poets of Greece and Rome introduce the dragon into their fables, as an illustration, when the type of power and ferocity is sought for. Homer, in his description of the shield of Hercules, speaks of "The scaly horror of a dragon coiled full in the central field, unspeakable, with eyes oblique, retorted, that askant shot gleaming fire." So Hesiod, describing the same object, says : "On its centre was the unspeakable terror of a dragon glancing backward with eyes gleaming with fire. His mouth, too, was filled with teeth running in a white line, dread and unapproachable ; and above his terrible forehead, dread strife was hovering, as he raises the battle rout. On it likewise were heads of terrible serpents, unspeakable, twelve in number, who were wont to scare the race of men on earth, whosoever chanced to wage war against the son of Jove."

Here it is noteworthy that Hesiod distinguishes between the dragon and serpents.

Ovid (41) locates the dragon slain by Cadmus in Bœotia, near the river Cephisus. He speaks of it as being hid in a cavern, adorned with crests, and of a golden colour. He, like the other poets, makes special reference to the eyes sparkling with fire, and it may be noted that a similar brilliancy is mentioned by those who have observed pythons in their native condition. He speaks of the dragon as blue, and terribly destructive owing to the possession of a sting, long constricting folds, and venomous breath.

The story of Ceres flying to heaven in a chariot drawn by two dragons, and of her subsequently lending it to Triptolemus, to enable him to travel all over the earth and distribute corn to its inhabitants, is detailed or alluded to by numerous poets, as well as the tale of Medea flying from Jason in a chariot drawn by winged dragons. Ceres (42) is further made to skim the waves of the ocean, much after the fashion of mythical personages depicted in the wood-cuts illustrating passages in the Shan Hai King. Ammianus Marcellinus, whose history ends with the death of Valerius in A.D. 378, refers, as a remarkable instance of credulity, to a vulgar rumour that the chariot of Triptolemus was still extant, and had enabled Julian, who had rendered himself formidable by sea and land, to pass over the walls of, and enter into the city of Heraclea. Though rational explanations are afforded by the theory of Bochart and Le Clerc, that the story is based upon the equivocal meaning of a Phoenician word, signifying either a winged dragon or a ship fastened with iron nails or bolts : or by that of Philodorus, as cited by Eusebius, who says that his ship was called a flying dragon, from its carrying the figure of a dragon on its prow ; yet either simply transposes into another phase the current belief in a dragon, without prejudicing it.

Diodorus Siculus disposes of the Colchian dragon and the golden-fleeced ram in a very summary manner, as follows : —

"It is said that Phryxus, the son of Athamas and Nephele, in order to escape the snares of his stepmother, fled from Greece with his half-sister Hellen, and that whilst they were being carried, under the advice of the gods, by the ram with a golden fleece out of Europe into Asia, the girl accidentally fell off into the sea, which on that account has been called Hellespont. Phryxus, however, being carried safely into Colchis, sacrificed the ram by the order of an oracle, and hung up its skin in a shrine dedicated to Mars.

"After this the king learnt from an oracle that he would meet his death when strangers, arriving there by ship, should have carried off the golden fleece. On this account, as well as from innate cruelty, the man was induced to offer sacrifice with the slaughter of his guests ; in order that, the report of such an atrocity being spread everywhere, no one might dare to set foot within his dominions. He also surrounded the temple with a wall, and placed there a strong guard of Taurian soldiery ; which gave rise to a prodigious fiction among the Greeks, for it was reported by them that bulls, breathing fire from their nostrils, kept watch over the shrine, and that a dragon guarded the skin, for by ambiguity the name of the Taurians was twisted into that of bulls, and the slaughter of guests furnished the fiction of the expiation of fire. In like manner they translated the name of the prefect Draco, to whom the custody of the temple had been assigned, into that of the monstrous and horrible creature of the poets."

Nor do others fail to give a similar explanation of the fable of Phryxus, for they say that Phryxus was conveyed in a ship which bore on its prow the image of a ram, and that Hellen, who was leaning over the side under the misery of sea-sickness, tumbled into the water.

Among other subjects of poetry are the dragon which guarded the golden apples of the Hesperides, and the two which licked the eyes of Plutus at the temple of Æsculapius with such happy effect that he began to see.

Philostratus separates dragons into Mountain dragons and Marsh dragons. The former had a moderate crest, which increased as they grew older, when a beard of saffron colour was appended to their chins ; the marsh dragons had no crests. He speaks of their attaining a size so enormous that they easily killed elephants. Ælian describes their length as being from thirty or forty to a hundred cubits ; and Posidonius mentions one, a hundred and forty feet long, that haunted the neighbourhood of Damascus ; and another, whose lair was at Macra, near Jordan, was an acre in length, and of such bulk that two men on horseback, with the monster between them, could not see each other.

Ignatius states that there was in the library of Constantinople the intestine of a dragon one hundred and twenty feet long, on which were written the 'Iliad' and 'Odyssey' in letters of gold. There is no ambiguity in Lucan's (43) description of the Ethiopian dragon : "You also, the dragon, shining with golden brightness, who crawl in all (other) lands as innoxious divinities, scorching Africa, render deadly with wings ; you move the air on high, and

32

The ' vaporous and venomous breath ' of the terrestrial dragon, which could bring down a bird in flight, has here become the sulphurous breath which belches from the Hell-mouth, drawing down the bodies of the damned.   And the coils of the earthly serpent, used to such good effect against the beasts of the forest, now fasten on the souls of sinners. For the dragon, in Christian mythology, is a creature of Hell — at times the Devil himself: at others a symbol of Satan, displayed in the natural world, as living evidence to Man of the evil which besets his life on earth, and threatens his hope of future bliss in Heaven.

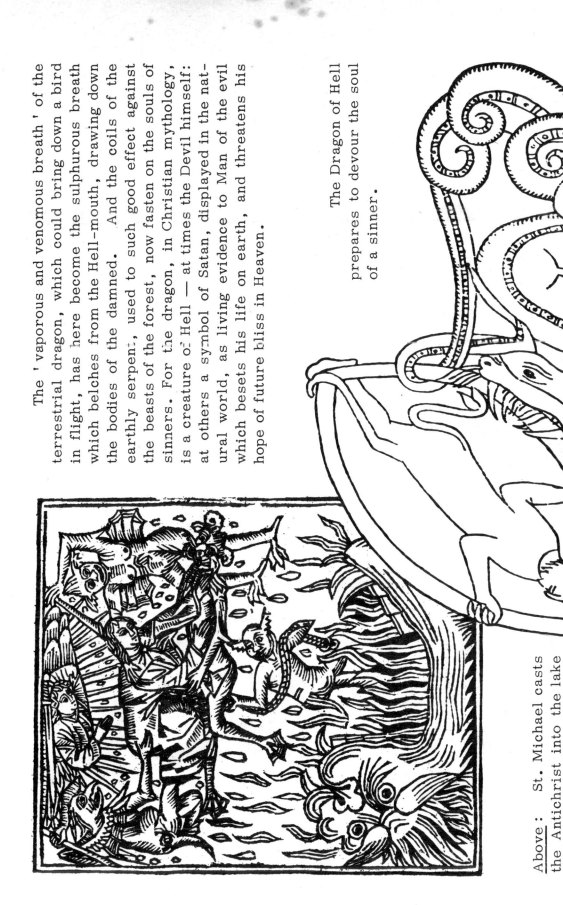

The Dragon of Hell prepares to devour the soul of a sinner.

Above : St. Michael casts the Antichrist into the lake of fire and brimstone. From 'El Libro del Antechristo'.

PLATE THREE

33

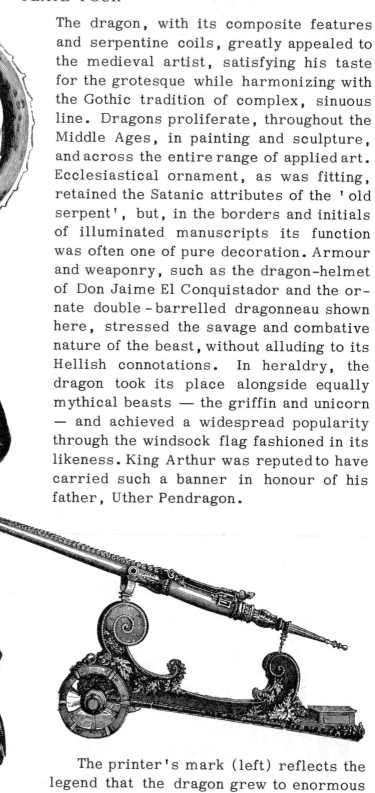

The dragon, with its composite features and serpentine coils, greatly appealed to the medieval artist, satisfying his taste for the grotesque while harmonizing with the Gothic tradition of complex, sinuous line. Dragons proliferate, throughout the Middle Ages, in painting and sculpture, and across the entire range of applied art. Ecclesiastical ornament, as was fitting, retained the Satanic attributes of the 'old serpent', but, in the borders and initials of illuminated manuscripts its function was often one of pure decoration. Armour and weaponry, such as the dragon-helmet of Don Jaime El Conquistador and the ornate double-barrelled dragonneau shown here, stressed the savage and combative nature of the beast, without alluding to its Hellish connotations. In heraldry, the dragon took its place alongside equally mythical beasts — the griffin and unicorn — and achieved a widespread popularity through the windsock flag fashioned in its likeness. King Arthur was reputed to have carried such a banner in honour of his father, Uther Pendragon.

The printer's mark (left) reflects the legend that the dragon grew to enormous size by feeding on others of a similarly poisonous nature.

following whole herds, you burst asunder vast bulls, embracing them with your folds. Nor is the elephant safe through his size ; everything you devote to death, and no need have you of venom for a deadly fate." Whereas the dragon referred to by Pliny, as also combating the elephant, is evidently without wings, and may either have been a very gigantic serpent, or a lacertian corresponding to the Chinese idea of the dragon.

Descending to later periods, we learn from Marcellinus (44) that in his day dragon standards were among the chief insignia of the Roman army ; for, speaking of the triumphal entry of Constantine into Rome after his triumph over Magnentius, he mentions that numbers of the chief officers who preceeded him were surrounded by dragons embroidered on various points of tissue, fastened to the golden or jewelled points of spears ; the mouths of the dragons being open so as to catch the wind, which made them hiss as though they were inflamed with anger, while the coils of their tails were also contrived to be agitated by the breeze. And again he speaks of Silvanus (45) tearing the purple silk from the insignia of the dragons and standards, and so assuming the title of Emperor.

Several nations, as the Persians, Parthians, Scythians, etc., bore dragons on their standards ; whence the standards themselves were called dracones or dragons.

It is probable that the Romans borrowed this custom from the Parthians, or, as Casaubon has it, from the Dacae, or Codin, from the Assyrians ; but while the Roman dracones were, as we learn from Ammianus Marcellinus, figures of dragons painted in red on their flags, among the Persians and Parthians they were, like the Roman eagles, figures in relievo, so that the Romans were frequently deceived and took them for real dragons.

The dragon plays an important part in Celtic mythology. Among the Celts, as with the Romans, it was the national standard.

> While Cymri's dragon, from the Roman's hold
> Spread with calm wing o'er Carduel's domes of gold. (46)

The fables of Merllin, Nennius, and Geoffrey describe it as red in colour, and so differing from the Saxon dragon which was white. The hero Arthur carried a dragon on his helm, and the tradition of it is moulded into imperishable form in the 'Faerie Queen'. A dragon infested Lludd's dominion, and made every heath in England resound with shrieks on each May-day eve. A dragon of vast size and pestiferous breath lay hidden in a cavern in Wales, and destroyed two districts with its venom, before the holy St. Samson seized and threw it into the sea.

In Celtic chivalry, the word dragon came to be used for chief, a Pen-dragon being a sort of dictator created in times of danger ; and as the knights who slew a chief in battle were said to slay a dragon, this doubtless helped to keep alive the popular tradition regarding the monster which had been carried with them westward in their migration from the common Aryan centre.

The Teutonic tribes who invaded and settled in England bore the effigies of dragons on their shields and banners, and these were also depicted on the ensigns of various German tribes. We also find that Thor himself was a slayer of dragons, and both Siegfried and Beowulf were similarly engaged in the Niebelungen-lied and the epic bearing the name of the latter. The Berserkers not only named their boats after the dragon, but also had the prow ornamented with a dragon figure-head ; a fashion which obtains to the present day among the Chinese, who have an annual dragon-boat festival, in which long snaky boats with a ferocious dragon prow run races for prizes, and paddle in processions.

So deeply associated was the dragon with the popular legends, that we find stories of encounters with it passing down into the literature of the Middle Ages ; and, like the heroes of old, the Christian saints won their principal renown by dragon achievements. Thus among the dragon-slayers we find that —

1. St. Phillip the Apostle destroyed a huge dragon at Hierapolis in Phrygia.
2. St. Martha killed the terrible dragon called Tarasque at Aix (la Chapelle).
3. St. Florent killed a similar dragon which haunted the Loire.
4. St. Cado, St. Mandet, and St. Paul did similar feats in Brittany.
5. St. Keyne of Cornwall slew a dragon.
6. St. Michael, St. George, St. Margaret, Pope Sylvester, St. Samson, Archbishop of Dol, Donatus (fourth century), St. Clement of Metz, killed dragons.
7. St. Romain of Rouen destroyed the huge dragon called La Gargouille, which ravaged the Seine.

Moreover, the fossil remains of animals discovered from time to time, and now relegated to their true position in the zoological series, were supposed to be the genuine remains of either dragons or giants, according to the bent of the mind of the individual who stumbled on them ; much as in the present day large fossil bones of extinct animals of all kinds are in China ascribed to dragons, and form an important item in the Chinese pharmaco-pœia. (Vide extract on Dragon bones from the Pen-tsaou-kang-mu, given on pp. 88-89).

Among the latest surviving beliefs of this nature may be cited the dragon of Wantley (Wharncliffe, Yorkshire), who was slain by More of More Hall. He procured a suit of armour studded with spikes, and, proceeding to the well where the dragon had his lair, kicked him in the mouth, where alone he was vulnerable. The Lambton worm is another instance.

The explanations of these legends attempted by mythologists, based on the supposition that the dragons which are their subjects are simply symbolic of natural phenomena, are ingenious, and perhaps in many instances sufficient, but do not affect, as I have before remarked, the primitive and conserved belief in their previous existence as a reality.

Thus, the author of 'British Goblins' suggests that for the prototype of the red dragon, which haunted caverns and guarded treasures in Wales, we must look in the lightning caverns of old Aryan fable, and deduces the fire-darting dragons of modern lore from the shining hammer of Thor, and the lightning spear of Odin.

The stories of ladies guarded by dragons are explained on the supposition that the ladies were kept in the secured part of the feudal castles, round which the walls wound, and that an adventurer had to scale the walls to gain access to the ladies ; when there were two walls, the authors of romance said that the assaulter overcame two dragons, and so on. St. Romain, when he delivered the city of Rouen from a dragon which lived in the river Seine, simply protected the city from an overflow, just as Apollo (the sun) is symbolically said to have destroyed the serpent Python, or, in other words, dried up an overflow. And the dragon of Wantley is supposed by Dr. Percy to have been an overgrown rascally attorney, who cheated some children of their estates, but was compelled to disgorge by a gentleman named More, who went against him armed with the " spikes of the law ", whereupon the attorney died of vexation.

Furthermore, our dragons were so denominated because they were armed with dragons, that is, with short muskets, which spouted fire like dragons, and had the head of a dragon wrought upon their muzzle.

This fanciful device occurs also among the Chinese, for a Jesuit, who accompanied the Emperor of China on a journey into Western Tartary in 1683, says, "This was the reason of his coming into their country with so great an army, and such vast military preparations ; he having commanded several pieces of cannon to be brought, in order for them to be discharged from time to time in the valleys ; purposely that the noise and fire, issuing from the mouths of the dragons, with which they were adorned, might spread terror around."

Though dragons have completely dropped out of all modern works on
natural history, they were still retained and regarded as quite orthodox until
a little before the time of Cuvier ; specimens, doubtless fabricated like the
ingeniously constructed mermaid of Mr. Barnum, were exhibited in the mus-
eums ; and voyagers occasionally brought back, as authentic stories of their
existence, fables which had percolated through time and nations until they had
found a home in people so remote from their starting point as to cause a complete obliteration of their passage and origin.

For instance, Pigafetta, in a report of the kingdom of Congo (47),
"gathered out of the discourses of Mr. E. Lopes, a Portuguese", speaking of
the province of Bemba, which he defines as "on the sea coast from the river
Ambrize, until the river Coanza towards the south", says of serpents,
"There are also certain other creatures which, being as big as rams, have
wings like dragons, with long tails, and long chaps, and divers rows of teeth,
and feed upon raw flesh. Their colour is blue and green, their skin painted
like scales, and they have two feet but no more. The Pagan negroes used to
worship them as gods, and at this day you may see divers of them that are
kept for a marvel. And because they are very rare, the chief lords there
curiously preserve them, and suffer the people to worship them, which tendeth
greatly to their profits by reason of the gifts and oblations which the people
offer unto them."

And John Barbot, Agent-General of the Royal Company of Africa, in his
description of the coasts of South Guinea (48), says : "Some blacks assuring
me that they (i.e., snakes) were thirty feet long. They also told me there are
winged serpents or dragons having a forked tail and a prodigious wide mouth,
full of sharp teeth, extremely mischievous to mankind, and more particularly
to small children. If we may credit this account of the blacks, they are of the
same sort of winged serpents which some authors tell us are to be found in
Abyssinia, being very great enemies to the elephants. Some such serpents
have been seen about the river Senegal, and they are adorned and worshipped
as snakes are at Wida or Fida, that is, in a most religious manner."

Ulysses Aldrovandus (49), who published a large folio volume on
serpents and dragons, entirely believed in the existence of the latter, and
gives two wood engravings of a specimen which he professes to have received
in the year 1551, of a true dried Ethiopian dragon.

He describes it as having two feet armed with claws, and two ears,
with five prominent and conspicuous tubercles on the back. The whole was

ornamented with green and dusky scales. Above, it bore wings fit for flight, and had a long and flexible tail, coloured with yellowish scales, such as shone on the belly and throat. The mouth was provided with sharp teeth, the inferior part of the head, towards the ears, was even, the pupil of the eye black, with a tawny surrounding, and the nostrils were two in number, and open.

He criticises Ammianus Marcellinus for his disbelief in winged dragons, and states in further justification of his censure that he had heard, from men worthy of confidence, that in that portion of Pistorian territory called Cotone, a great dragon was seen whose wings were interwoven with sinews a cubit in length, and were of considerable width ; this beast also possessed two short feet provided with claws like those of an eagle. The whole animal was covered with scales. The gaping mouth was furnished with big teeth, it had ears, and was as big as a hairy bear. Aldrovandus sustains his argument by quotations from the classics and reference to more recent authors. He quotes Isidorus as stating that the winged Arabian serpents were called Sirens, while their venom was so effective that their bite was attended by death rather than pain ; this confirms the account of Solinus.

He instances Gesner as saying that, in 1543, he understood that a kind of dragon appeared near Styria, within the confines of Germany, which had feet like lizards, and wings after the fashion of a bat, with an incurable bite, and says these statements are confirmed by Froschonerus in his work on Styria. He classes dragons (which he considers as essentially winged animals) either as footless or possessing two or four feet.

He refers to a description by Scaliger of a species of serpent four feet long, and as thick as a man's arm, with cartilaginous wings pendent from the sides. He also mentions an account by Brodeus, of a winged dragon which was brought to Francis, the invincible King of the Gauls, by a countryman who had killed it with a mattock near Sanctones, and which was stated to have been seen by many men of approved reputation, who thought it had migrated from trans-marine regions by the assistance of the wind.

Cardan (50) states that whilst he resided in Paris he saw five winged dragons in the William Museum ; these were biped, and possessed of wings so slender that it was hardly possible that they could fly with them. Cardan doubted their having been fabricated, since they had been sent in vessels at different times, and yet all presented the same remarkable form. Bellonius states that he had seen whole carcases of winged dragons, carefully prepared, which he considered to be of the same kind as those which fly out of Arabia into Egypt ; they were thick about the belly, had two feet, and two wings, whole like those of a bat, and a snake's tail.

It would be useless to multiply examples of the stories, no doubt fables, current in medieval times, and I shall therefore only add here two of those which, though little known, are probably fair samples of the whole. It is amusing to find the story of Sinbad's escape from the Valley of Diamonds re-appearing in Europe during the Middle Ages, with a substitution of the dragon for the roc. Athanasius Kircher, in the 'Mundus Subterraneus', gives the story of a Lucerne man who, in wandering over Mount Pilate, tumbled into a cavern from which there was no exit, and, in searching round, discovered the lair of two dragons, who proved more tender than their reputation. Unharmed by them he remained for the six winter months, without any other sustenance than that which he derived from licking the moisture off the rock, in which he followed their example. Noticing the dragons preparing for flying out on the approach of spring, by stretching and unfolding their wings, he attached him-self by his girdle to the tail of one of them, and so was restored to the upper world, where, unfortunately, the return to the diet to which he had been so long unaccustomed killed him. In memory, however, of the event, he left his goods to the Church, and a monument illustrative of his escape was erected in the Ecclesiastical College of St. Leodegaris at Lucerne. Kircher had himself seen this, and it was accepted as an irrefragable proof of the story.

Another story is an account also given by Kircher, of the fight between a dragon and a knight named Gozione, in the island of Rhodes, in the year 1349 A.D. This monster is described as of the bulk of a horse or ox, with a long neck and serpent's head — tipped with mule's ears — the mouth widely gaping and furnished with sharp teeth, eyes sparkling as though they flashed fire, four feet provided with claws like a bear, and a tail like a crocodile, the whole body being coated with hard scales. It had two wings, blue above, but blood-coloured and yellow underneath ; it was swifter than a horse, progressing partly by flight and partly by running. The knight, being solicited by the chief magistrate, retired into the country, where he constructed an imitation dragon of paper and tow, and purchased a charger and two courageous English dogs ; he ordered slaves to snap the jaws and twist the tail about by means of cords, while he urged his horse and dogs on to the attack. After practising for two months, these latter could scarcely retain their frenzy at the mere sight of the image. He then proceeded to Rhodes, and after offering his vows in the Church of St. Stephen, repaired to the fatal cave, instructing his slaves to witness the combat from a lofty rock, and hasten to him with remedies, if after slaying the dragon he should be overcome by the poisonous exhalations, or to save themselves in the event of his being slain. Entering the lair he excited the beast with shouts and cries, and then awaited it outside. The dragon appearing, allured by the expectation of an easy prey, rushed on him, both running and flying ; the knight shattered his spear at the first onset on the scaly carcase, and leaping from his horse continued the contest with sword and shield. The dragon, raising itself on its hind legs, endeavoured to grasp the knight with his fore ones, giving the latter an opportunity of striking him in the softer parts of the neck. At last both fell together, the knight being exhausted by the fatigue of the conflict, or by mephitic exhalations. The slaves, according to instruction, rushed forward, dragged off the monster from their master, and fetched water in their caps to restore him ; after which he mounted his horse and returned in triumph to the city, where he was at first ungratefully received, but afterwards rewarded with the highest ranks of the order, and created magistrate of the province.

Kircher had a very pious belief in dragons. He says : "Since monstrous animals of this kind for the most part select their lairs and breeding-places in subterraneous caverns, I have considered it proper to include them under the head of subterraneous beasts. I am aware that two kinds of this animal have been distinguished by authors, the one with, the other without, wings. No one either can or ought to doubt concerning the latter kind of creature, unless perchance he dares to contradict the Holy Scripture, for it would be an impious thing to say it when Daniel makes mention of the divine worship accorded to the dragon Bel by the Babylonians, and after the mention of the dragon made in other parts of the sacred writings."

Harris, in his 'Collection of Voyages', gives a singular resume. He says : "We have, in an ancient author, a very large and circumstantial account of the taking of a dragon on the frontiers of Ethiopia, which was one and twenty feet in length, and was carried to Ptolemy Philadelphus, who very bountifully rewarded such as ran the hazard of procuring him this beast. (Diodorus Siculus, lib.iii.) ... Yet terrible as these were they fall abundantly short of monsters of the same species in India, with respect to which St. Ambrose (51) tells us that there were dragons seen in the neighbourhood of the Ganges nearly seventy cubits in length. It was one of this size that Alexander and his army saw in a cave, where it was fed, either out of reverence or from curiosity, by the inhabitants ; and the first lightning of its eyes, together with its terrible hissing, made a strong impression on the Macedonians, who, with all their courage, could not help being frighted at so horrid a spectacle (52). The dragon is nothing more than a serpent of enormous size ; and they formerly distinguished three sorts of them in the Indies, viz. such as were found in the mountains, such as were bred in caves or in the flat country, and such as were found in fens and marshes.

"The first is the largest of all, and are covered with scales as resplendent as polished gold. These have a kind of beard hanging from their lower jaw, their eyebrows large, and very exactly arched ; their aspect the most frightful that can be imagined, and their cry loud and shrill ; their crests of a bright yellow, and a protuberance on their heads of the colour of a burning coal.

"Those of the flat country differ from the former in nothing but in having their scales of a silver colour, and in their frequenting rivers, to which the former never come.

"Those that live in marshes and fens are of a dark colour, approaching to a black, move slowly, have no crest, or any rising upon their heads. Strabo says that the painting them with wings is the effect of fancy, and directly contrary to truth, but other naturalists and travellers both ancient and modern affirm that there are some of these species winged. Pliny says their bite is not venomous, other authors deny this. Pliny gives a long catalogue of medical and magical properties, which he ascribes to the skin, flesh, bones, eyes, and teeth of the dragon, also a valuable stone in its head. ' They hung before the mouth of the dragon den a piece of stuff flowered with gold, which attracted the eyes of the beast, till by the sound of soft music they lulled him to sleep, and then cut off his head '."

I do not find Harris's statement in Diodorus Siculus, the author quoted, but there is the very circumstantial description of a serpent thirty cubits (say forty-five feet) in length, which was captured alive by stratagem, the first attempt by force having resulted in the death of several of the party. This was conveyed to Ptolemy II at Alexandria, where it was placed in a den or chamber suitable for exhibition, and became an object of general admiration. Diodorus says : "When, therefore, so enormous a serpent was open for all to see, credence could no longer be refused the Ethiopians, or their statements be received as fables ; for they say that they have seen in their country serpents so vast that they can not only swallow cattle and other beasts of the same size, but that they also fight with the elephant, embracing his limbs so tightly in the fold of their coils that he is unable to move, and, raising their neck up underneath his trunk, direct their head against the elephant's eyes ; having destroyed his sight by fiery rays like lightning, they dash him to the ground, and, having done so, tear him to pieces."

In an account of the castle of Fahender, formerly one of the most considerable castles of Fars, it is stated — "Such is the historical foundation of an opinion generally prevalent, that the subterranean recesses of this deserted edifice are still replete with riches. The talisman has not been forgotten ; and tradition adds another guardian to the previous deposit, a dragon or winged serpent ; this sits for ever brooding over the treasure which it cannot enjoy."

43

When the body of Cleomenes was crucified, and hung upon the Crosse, it is reported by them that were the watch - men about it, that there came a Dragon and did winde it self about his body, and with his head covered the face of the dead King, oftentimes licking the same, and not suffering any Bird to come neer and touch the carkasse. For which cause there began to be a reverent opinion of divinity attributed to the king, until such time as wise and prudent men, studious of the truth, found out the true cause hereof. For they say that as Bees are generated out of the body of Oxen, and Drones of Horses, and Hornets of Asses : so do the bodies of men ingender out of their marrow a Serpent, and for this cause the Ancients were moved to consecrate the Dragon to Noble-spirited men.

Edward Topsell,
THE HISTORY OF SERPENTS,
London, 1658.

APPENDIX 1

AElian : De Natura Animalium : —

Book II. ch. 26.

The dragon (which is perfectly fearless of beasts), when it hears the noise of the wings of an eagle, immediately conceals itself in hiding-places.

Book II. ch. 21.

Ethiopia generates dragons reaching thirty paces long ; they have no proper name, but they merely call them slayers of elephants, and they attain a great age. So far do the Ethiopian accounts narrate. The Phrygian history also states that dragons are born which reach ten paces in length ; which daily in midsummer, at the hour when the forum is full of men in assembly, are wont to proceed from their caverns, and (near the river Rhyndacus), with part of the body on the ground, and the rest erect, with the neck gently stretched out, and gaping mouth, attract birds, either by their inspiration, or by some fascination, and that those which are drawn down by the inhalation of their breath glide down into their stomach — (and that they continue this until sunset) but that after that, concealing themselves, they lay in ambush for the herds returning from the pasture to the stable, and inflict much injury, often killing the herdsmen and gorging themselves with food.

Book VI. ch. 4.

When dragons are about to eat fruit they suck the juice of the wild chicory, because this affords them a sovereign remedy against inflation. When they purpose lying in wait for a man or a beast, they eat deadly roots and herbs ; a thing not unknown to Homer, for he makes mention of the dragon, who, lingering and twisting himself in front of his den, devoured noxious herbs.

Book VI. ch. 21.

In India, as I am told, there is great enmity between the dragon and elephant. Wherefore the dragons, aware that elephants are accustomed to pluck off boughs from trees for food, coil themselves beforehand in these trees, folding the tail half of their body round the limbs, and leaving the front half hanging like a rope. When an elephant approaches for the purpose of browsing on the young branches, the dragon leaping upon him, tears out his eyes, and then squeezing his neck with his front part and lashing him with his tail, strangles him in this strange kind of noose.

Book VI. ch. 22.

The elephant has a great horror of the dragon.

Book VI. ch. 17.

In Idumea, or Judea, during Herod's power, according to the statement of the natives of the country, a very beautiful, and just adolescent, woman, was beloved by a dragon of exceptional magnitude ; who visited her betimes and slept with her as a lover. She, indeed, although her lover crept towards her as gently and quietly as lay in his power, yet utterly alarmed, withdrew herself from him ; and to the end that a forgetfulness of his passion might result from the absence of his mistress, absented herself for the space of a month.

But the desire of the absent one was increased in him, and his amatory dis-position was daily so far aggravated that he frequently came both by day and night to that spot, where he had been wont to be with the maiden, and when unable to meet with his inamorata, was afflicted with a terrible grief. After the girl returned, angry at being, as it were, spurned, he coiled himself round her body, and softly and gently chastised her legs.

Book VI. ch. 63.

A dragon whelp, born in Arcadia, was brought up with an Arcadian child ; and in process of time, when both were older, they entertained a mutual affection for one another. The friends of the boy, seeing how the dragon had increased in magnitude in so short a time, carried him, while sleeping with the boy in the same bed, to a remote spot, and, leaving him there, brought the boy back. The dragon thereon remained in the wood (feeding on growing plants and poisons), preferring a solitary life to one in towns and (human) habitations. Time having rolled on, and the boy having attained youth, and the dragon maturity, the former, while travelling upon one occasion through the wilds in the neighbourhood of his friend, fell among robbers, who attacked him with drawn swords, and being struck, either from pain, or in the hopes of assistance, cried out. The dragon being a beast of acute hearing and sharp vision, as soon as he heard the lad with whom he had been brought up, gave a hiss in expression of his anger, and so struck them with fear, that the trem-bling robbers dispersed in different directions, whom having caught, he des-troyed by a terrible death. Afterwards, having cared for the wounds of his ancient friend, and escorted him through the places infested with serpents, he returned to the spot where he himself had been exposed — not showing any anger towards him on account of his having been expelled into solitude, nor because ill-feeling men had abandoned an old friend in danger.

Book VIII. ch. 11.

Hegemon, in his Dardanic verses, among other things mentions, concern-ing the Thessalian Alevus, that a dragon conceived an affection for him. Alevus possessed, as Hegemon states, golden hair, which I should call yellow, and pastured cattle upon Ossa near the Thessalian spring called Haemonium (as

Anchises formerly did on Ida). A dragon of great size fell violently in love with him, and used to crawl up gently to him, kiss his hair, cleanse his face by licking it with his tongue, and bring him various spoils from the chase.

Book X. ch. 25.

Beyond the Oasis of Egypt there is a great desert which extends for seven days' journey, succeeded by a region inhabited by the Cynoprosopi, on the way to Ethiopia. These live by the chase of goats and antelopes. They are black, with the head and teeth of a dog, of which animal, in this connection, the mention is not to be looked upon as absurd, for they lack the power of speech, and utter a shrill hissing sound, and have a beard above and below the mouth like a dragon ; their hands are armed with strong and sharp nails, and the body is equally hairy with that of dogs.

Book X. ch. 48.

Lycaonus, King of Emathia, had a son named Macedon, from whom eventually the country was called, the old name becoming obsolete. Now, one of Macedon's sons, named Pindus, was indued both with strength of mind and innate probity, as well as a handsome person, whereas his other children were constituted with mean minds and less vigorous bodies.

When, therefore, these latter perceived Pindus's virtue and other gifts, they not only oppressed him, but in the end ruined themselves in punishment for so great a crime.

Pindus, perceiving that plots were laid for him by his brothers, abandoning the kingdom which he had received from his father, and being robust and taking pleasure in hunting, not only took to it himself, but led others to follow his example.

Upon one occasion he was pursuing some young mules, and, spurring his horse to the top of its powers, drew away a long distance from those who were hunting with him. The mules passing into a deep cavern, escaped the sight of their pursuer, and preserved themselves from danger. He leaped down from the horse, which he tied to the nearest tree, and whilst he was seeking with his utmost ability to discover the mules, and probing the dens with his hands, heard a voice warning him not to touch the mules. Wherefore, when he had long and carefully looked about, and could see no one, he feared that the voice was the result of some greater cause, and, mounting his horse, left the place. On the next day he returned to the spot, but, deterred by the remembrance of the voice he had heard, he did not enter the place where they had concealed themselves.

When, therefore, he was cogitating as to who had warned him from following his prey, and, as it appeared, was looking out for mountain shepherds, or hunters, or some cottage — a dragon of unusual magnitude appeared to him, creeping softly with a great part of its body, but raising up its neck and head

47

a little way, as if stretching himself — but his neck and head were of such height as to equal that of the tallest man.

Although Pindus was alarmed at the sight, he did not take to flight, but, rallying himself from his great terror, wisely endeavoured to appease the beast by giving him to eat the birds he had caught, as the price of his redemption.

He, cajoled by the gifts and baits, or, as I may say, touched, left the spot. This was so pleasing to Pindus, that, as an honourable man, and grateful for his escape, he carried to the dragon, as a thank-offering, whatever he could procure from his mountain chases, or by fowling.

Nor were these gifts from his booty without return, for fortune became immediately more favourable to him, and he achieved success in all his hunting whether he pursued ground or winged game.

Wherefore he achieved a great reputation, both for finding and quickly catching game.

Now, he was so tall that he caused terror from his bulk, while from his excellent constitution and beautiful countenance he inflamed women with so violent an affection for him, that the unmarried, as if they were furious and bacchantes, joined his hunting expeditions ; and married women, under the guardianship of husbands, preferred passing their time with him, to being reported among the number of goddesses. And, for the most part, men also esteemed him highly, as his virtue and appearance attracted universal admiration. His brothers only held a hostile and inimical feeling towards him. Wherefore upon a certain occasion they attacked him from an ambush, when he was hunting alone, and having driven him into the defiles of a river close by, when he was removed from all help, attacked him with drawn swords and slew him.

When the dragon heard its friend's outcries (for it is an animal with as sharp a sense of hearing as it has quickness of vision), it issued from its lair, and at once, casting its coils round the impious wretches, suffocated them.

It did not desist from watching over its slain (friend) with the utmost care, until those nearest related to the deceased came to him, as he was lying on the ground ; but nevertheless, although clad in proper mourning, they were prevented through fear of the custodian from approaching and interring the dead with proper rites, until it, understanding from its profound and wonderful nature, that it was keeping them at a distance, quietly departed from its guard and station near the body, in order that it might receive the last tokens of esteem from the bystanders without any interruption.

Splendid obsequies were performed, and the river where the murder was effected received its name from the dead man.

It is therefore a peculiarity of these beasts to be grateful to those from whom they may have received favours.

Book XI. ch. 2. — Dragon Sacred to Apollo

The Epirotes, both at home and abroad, sacrifice to Apollo, and solemnise with extreme magnificence a feast yearly in his honour. There is a grove among them sacred to the god, and inclosed with a wall, within which are dragons, pleasing to the god. Hither a sacred virgin comes alone, naked, and presents food to the dragons. The Epirotes say that these are descended from the Delphic python. If they regarded the virgin ministering to them with favour, and took the food promptly, they were believed to portend a fertile and healthful year ; if they were rude towards her, and would not accept the proferred food, some predicted, or at least expected, the contrary for the coming year.

Book II. ch. 16. — Dragon in Lavinium.

There is a peculiar divination of the dragon, for in Lavinium, a town of the Latins but in Lavinium, there is a large and dense sacred grove, and near it the shrine of the Argolic Juno. Within the grove is a cave and deep den, the lair of a dragon.

Sacred virgins enter this grove on stated days, who carry a barley cake in their hands, with bandaged eyes. A certain divine afflatus leads them accurately to the den, and gently, and step by step, they proceed without hindrance, and as if their eyes were uncovered. If they are virgins, the dragon admits the food as pure and fit for a deity. If otherwise, it does not touch it, perceiving and divining them to be impure.

Ants, for the sake of cleansing the place, carry from the grove the cake left by the vitiated virgin, broken into little pieces, so that they may easily carry it. When this happens, it is perceived by the inhabitants, and those who have entered are pointed out and examined, and whoever proves to have forfeited her virginity is punished with the penalties appointed by the laws.

"The masculine sex also seems to be privileged by nature among brutes, inasmuch as the male dragon is distinguished by a crest and hairs, with a beard."

Book XVI. ch. 39.

Onesicritus Astypalaeus writes that there were two dragons in India (nurtured by an Indian dancer), one of forty-six and the other of eighty cubits, and that Alexander (Philip's son) earnestly endeavoured to see them. It is affirmed in Egyptian books that, during the reign of Philadelphus, two dragons were brought from Ethiopia into Philadelphia alive, one forty, the other thirty cubits in magnitude.

Three were also brought in the time of King Evergetis, one nine and another seven cubits. The Egyptians say that the third was preserved with great care in the temple of Æsculapius.

It is also said that there are asps of four cubits in length. Those who write the history of the affairs of Chios say that a dragon of extreme magnitude was produced in a valley, densely crowded and gloomy with tall trees, of the Mount Pelienaeus in that island, whose hissing struck the Chians with horror.

As none either of the husbandmen or shepherds dare, by approaching near, estimate its magnitude, but from its hissing judged it to be a large and form-idable beast, at length its size became known by a remarkable accident. For the trees of the valley being struck by a very strong wind, and the branches ignited by the friction, a great fire thence arising, embraced the whole spot, and surrounded the beast, which, being unable to escape, was consumed by the ardour of the flame. By these means all things were rendered visible in the denuded place, and the Chians, freed from their alarms, came to investigate, and lighted on bones of unusual magnitude, and an immense head, from which they were enabled to conjecture its dimensions when living.

Book XI. ch. 17.

Homer was not rash in his line,
> Terrible are the gods when they manifest themselves
For the dragon, while sacred and to be worshipped, has within himself something still more of the divine nature of which it is better to remain in ignorance.

Indeed, a dragon received divine honours in a certain tower in Melita in Egypt. He had his priests and ministers, his table and bowl. Every day they filled the bowl with flour kneaded with honey, and went away ; returning on the following day, they found the bowl empty.

Upon one occasion, a man of illustrious birth, who entertained an intense desire of seeing the dragon, having entered alone, and placed the food, went out ; and when the dragon commenced to feed at the table, he opened suddenly and noisily the doors, which according to custom he had closed.

The dragon indignantly left ; but he who had desired to see him, to his own destruction, being seized with an affliction of the mind, and having confessed his crime, presently lost his speech, and shortly after died.

Book XII. ch. 39.

When Halia, the daughter of Sybasis, had entered the grove of Diana in Phrygia, a certain sacred dragon of large size appeared and copulated with her ; whence the Ophiogenae deduce the origin of their race.

Book XV. ch. 21. — Concerning the Indian Dragon.

Alexander (while he attacked or devastated some portions of India, and also seized others) lighted on, among other numerous animals, a dragon, which the Indians, because they considered it to be sacred, and worshipped it with great reverence, in a certain cave, besought him with many entreaties to let alone, which he agreed to. However, when the dragon heard the noise made by the passing army (for it is an animal endowed with a very acute sense of hearing as well as of vision), it frightened and alarmed them all with a great hissing and blowing. It was said to be seventy cubits long.

It did not, however, show the whole of itself, but only exposed its head from the cave. Its eyes were said to have been of the size (and rotundity) of a Macedonian shield.

APPENDIX 2

S. Baring-Gould, 'Saint George ' (Extract), from the collection 'Curious Myths of the Middle Ages '.

The story of St. George and the dragon first presents itself in the Legenda Aurea of Jacques de Voragine. It was accepted by the unquestioning clerks and laity of the middle ages, so that it found its way into the office-books of the Church. The legend, as told by Voragine, is this : —

George, a tribune, was born in Cappadocia, and came to Lybia, to the town called Silene, near which was a pond infested by a monster, which had many times driven back an armed host that had come to destroy him. He even approached the walls of the city, and with his exhalations poisoned all who were near. To avoid such visits, he was furnished each day with two sheep, to satisfy his voracity. If these were not given, he so attacked the walls of the town, that his envenomed breath infected the air, and many of the inhabitants died. He was supplied with sheep, till they were exhausted, and it was impossible to procure the necessary number. Then the citizens held counsel, and it was decided that each day a man and a beast should be offered, so that at last they gave up their children, sons and daughters, and none were spared. The lot fell one day on the princess. The monarch, horror-struck, offered in exchange for her his gold, his silver, and half his realm, only desiring to save his daughter from this frightful death. But the people insisted on the sacrifice of the maiden, and all the poor father could obtain was a delay of eight days, in which to bewail the fate of the damsel. At the expiration of this time, the people returned to the palace, and said, "Why do you sacrifice your subjects for your daughter ? We are all dying before the breath of this monster ! " The king felt that he must resolve on parting with his child. He covered her with royal clothes, embraced her, and said, "Alas ! dear daughter, I thought to have seen myself reborn in your offspring. I hoped to have invited princes to your wedding, to have adorned you with royal garments, and accompanied you with flutes, tambourins, and all kinds of music ; but you are to be devoured by this monster ! Why did I not die before you ? "

Then she fell at her father's feet and besought his blessing. He accorded it
to her, weeping, and he clasped her tenderly in his arms ; then she went to the
lake. George, who passed that way, saw her weeping, and asked the cause of
her tears. She replied : — "Good youth ! quickly mount your horse and fly,
lest you perish with me." But George said to her : — "Do not fear ; tell me
what you await, and why all this multitude look on." She answered : — "I see
that you have a great and noble heart ; yet fly ! " "I shall not go without know-
ing the cause," he replied. Then she explained all to him ; whereupon he
exclaimed : — "Fear nothing ! in the name of Jesus Christ, I will assist you."
"Brave knight ! " said she ; "do not seek to die with me ; enough that I should
perish ; for you can neither assist nor deliver me, and you will only die with
me."

At this moment the monster rose above the surface of the water. And the
virgin said, all trembling, "Fly, fly, sir knight ! "

His only answer was the sign of the cross. Then he advanced to meet the
monster, recommending himself to God.

He brandished his lance with such force, that he transfixed it, and cast it
to the ground. Then, addressing the princess, he bade her pass her girdle
round it, and fear nothing. When this was done, the monster followed like a
docile hound. When they had brought it into the town, the people fled before it ;
but George recalled them, bidding them put aside all fear, for the Lord had
sent him to deliver them from the dragon. Then the king and all his people,
twenty thousand men, without counting women and children, were baptized,
and George smote off the head of the monster.

Other versions of the story are to the effect that the princess was shut up
in a castle, and that all within were perishing for want of water, which could
only be obtained from a fountain at the base of a hill, and this was guarded by
the "laidly worm", from which George delivered them.

The same story has attached itself to other saints and heroes of the middle
ages, as St. Secundus of Asti, St. Victor, Gozo of Rhodes, Raimond of St.
Sulpice, Struth von Winkelried, the Count Aymon, Moor of Moorhall "who slew
the dragon of Wantley", Conyers of Sockburn, and the Knight of Lambton,
"John that slew ye Worme." Ariosto adopted it into his "Orlando Furioso",
and made his hero deliver Angelica from Orca, in the true mythic style of
George ; and it appears again in the tale of Chederles. The cause of the legend
attaching itself to our hero was possibly a misunderstanding of an encomium,
made in memory of St. George, by Metaphrastes, which concludes thus : —
"Licebat igitur videre astutissimum Draconem, adversus carnem et sanguinem
gloriari solitum, elatumque, et sese efferentum, a juvene uno illusum, et ita
dispectum atque confusum, ut quid ageret non haberet." Another writer, sum-
ming up the acts of St. George, says : "Secundo quod Draconem vicit qui
significat Diabolum;" and Hospinian, relating the sufferings of the martyr,
affirms distinctly that his constancy was the occasion of the creation of the

The story of St. George, and of his struggle with the dragon, is far older than the faith which the Christian knight professed. The ancient Greeks told a similar tale of Perseus, who rescued the maiden Andromeda from a sea-monster. And, thousands of years before, the Babylonians recounted the legends of Bel, Enlil, and Marduk, who fought with the she-dragon Tiamat, so that the Cosmos might be saved from confusion. However the names and locations might change, the essential feature of the story remains the same in every age : The victory of Good over Evil, of Light over Darkness, of Order over Chaos.

Cadmus (above), the founder of Thebes, slays the dragon which guarded the Spring of Ares. In later life Cadmus himself was transformed into a serpent.

PLATE FIVE

53

PLATE SIX

Tiamat, the dragon-mother of the Babylonian pantheon and a personification of Chaos, is pursued by the chief of the gods, Marduk, who seeks her death so that order might be established in the universe. With the aid of a net, the bow of the rainbow, and a sheaf of lightnings, Marduk is able to destroy Tiamat and create heaven and earth from her body.

Herakles, in the garden of the Hesperides, confronts the ever-wakeful dragon Ladon who is set to guard over the golden apples of Hera. Like the multi-headed serpent, Hydra, already slain by Herakles in an earlier encounter, Ladon will be vanquished by the guile and strength of the hero.

Archangel St. Michael as dragon-slayer and Protector of the Church Militant of Christendom: 'And there was war in heaven : Michael and his angels fought against the dragon; and the dragon fought and his angels, and prevailed not .... And the great dragon was cast out, that old serpent, called the Devil, and Satan, which deceiveth the whole world...'

Several feats of dragon-slaying are included in the mythic traditions of northern Europe. Among the gods and heroes who performed the task are Thor, the Norse god who perished slaying the Midgard serpent ; Sigurd the Volsung, who killed the dragon Fafnir to obtain the treasure which it guarded ; and Siegfried, the Germanic hero who acquired both physical invulnerability and an understanding of the language of birds, after bathing in the blood of the slaughtered dragon Regin.

54

The story of St. George, and of his struggle with the dragon, is far older than the faith which the Christian knight professed. The ancient Greeks told a similar tale of Perseus, who rescued the maiden Andromeda from a sea-monster. And, thousands of years before, the Babylonians recounted the legends of Bel, Enlil, and Marduk, who fought with the she-dragon Tiamat, so that the Cosmos might be saved from confusion. However the names and locations might change, the essential feature of the story remains the same in every age : The victory of Good over Evil, of Light over Darkness, of Order over Chaos.

Cadmus (above), the founder of Thebes, slays the dragon which guarded the Spring of Ares. In later life Cadmus himself was trans-formed into a serpent.

PLATE FIVE

53

PLATE SIX

Tiamat, the dragon-mother of the Babylonian pantheon and a personification of Chaos, is pursued by the chief of the gods, Marduk, who seeks her death so that order might be established in the universe. With the aid of a net, the bow of the rainbow, and a sheaf of lightnings, Marduk is able to destroy Tiamat and create heaven and earth from her body.

Herakles, in the garden of the Hesperides, confronts the ever-wakeful dragon Ladon who is set to guard over the golden apples of Hera. Like the multi-headed serpent, Hydra, already slain by Herakles in an earlier encounter, Ladon will be vanquished by the guile and strength of the hero.

Archangel St. Michael as dragon-slayer and Protector of the Church Militant of Christendom: 'And there was war in heaven : Michael and his angels fought against the dragon; and the dragon fought and his angels, and prevailed not .... And the great dragon was cast out, that old serpent, called the Devil, and Satan, which deceiveth the whole world...'

Several feats of dragon-slaying are included in the mythic traditions of northern Europe. Among the gods and heroes who performed the task are Thor, the Norse god who perished slaying the Midgard serpent ; Sigurd the Volsung, who killed the dragon Fafnir to obtain the treasure which it guarded ; and Siegfried, the Germanic hero who acquired both physical invulnerability and an understanding of the language of birds, after bathing in the blood of the slaughtered dragon Regin.

54

legend by Voragine.

If we look at the story of Perseus and Andromeda, we shall find that in all essential particulars it is the same as that of the Cappadocian Saint.

Cassiope having boasted herself to be fairer than Hera, Poseidon sent a flood and a sea-monster to ravage the country belonging to her husband Cepheus. The oracle of Ammon having been consulted, it was ascertained that nothing would stop the resentment of the gods except the exposure of the king's daughter, Andromeda, on a rock, to be devoured by the monster. At the moment that the dragon approached the maiden, Perseus appeared, and learning her peril, engaged the monster and slew him.

The scene of this conflict was near Joppa, where in the days of St. Jerome the bones of the huge reptile were exhibited, and Josephus pretends to have seen there the chains which attached the princess to the rock. It was at Berytus (Beyrut) that the fight of St. George with the dragon took place.

Similar stories were prevalent in Greece. In the isle of Salamis, Cenchrius, a son of Poseidon, relieved the inhabitants from the scourge of a similar monster, who devastated the island. At Thespia, a dragon ravaged the country round the city ; Zeus ordered the inhabitants to give the monster their children by lot. One year it fell on Cleostratus. Menestratus determined to save him. He armed himself with a suit covered with hooks, and was devoured by the dragon, which perished in killing him. Pherecydes killed a great serpent in Caulonia, an adventure afterwards related of Pythagoras with the scene shifted to Sybaris ; and Herakles, as is well known, slew Hydra. But these are all versions — echoes — of the principal myth of Apollo and Python.

The monster Python was sent by Hera to persecute Leto, when pregnant. Apollo, the moment that he was born, attacked the hideous beast and pierced him with his arrows. And from the place where the serpent died, there burst forth a torrent.

A similar myth is found among the Scandinavian and Teutonic nations. In these Northern mythologies Apollo is replaced by Sigurd, Sigfried, and Beowulf.

The dragon with which Sigurd fights is Fafnir, who keeps guard over a treasure of gold. Sigfried, in like manner, in the Nibelungen Lied, fights and overcomes a mighty dragon, and despoils him of a vast treasure. The Anglo-Saxon poem of Beowulf contains a similar engagement. A monster, Grendel, haunts a marsh near a town on the North Sea. At night the evil spirit rises from the swamp, and flies to the mountains, attacking the armed men and slaying them. Beowulf awakes, fights him, and puts him to flight. But next night Grendel again attacks him, but is killed by the hero with an enchanted sword. He fights a dragon some years later, and robs it of an incalculable store of gold. The Icelandic Sagas teem with similar stories ; and they abound in all European house-hold tales.

In the Rigveda we have the same story. Indra fights with the hideous serpent Ahi, or Vrita, who keeps guard over the fountain of rains. In Iranian mythology, the same battle is waged between Mithra and the demon Ahriman.

It seems, then, that the fight with the dragon is a myth common to all Aryan peoples.

Its signification is this : —

The maiden which the dragon attempts to devour is the earth. The monster is the storm-cloud. The hero who fights it is the sun, with his glorious sword, the lightning-flash. By his victory the earth is relieved from her peril. The fable has been varied to suit the atmospheric peculiarities of different climes in which the Aryans found themselves. In India, Vrita is coiled about the source of water, and the earth is perishing for want of rain, till pierced by the sword of Indra, when the streams descend. "I will sing," says the Rigveda, "the ancient exploits by which flashing Indra is distinguished. He has struck Ahi, he has scattered the waters on the earth, he has unlocked the torrents of the heavenly mountains (i.e., the clouds). He has struck Ahi, who lurked in the bosom of the celestial mountain, he has struck him with that sounding weapon wrought for him by Twachtri ; and the waters, like cattle rushing to their stable, have poured down on the earth." And again : —

"O Indra, thou hast killed the violent Ahi, who withheld the waters ! "

"O Indra, thou hast struck Ahi, sleeping guardian of the waters, and thou hast precipitated them into the sea ; thou hast pierced the compact scale of the cloud ; thou hast given vent to the streams, which burst forth on all sides."

In the Katha Sarit Sagara, a hero fights a demon monster, and releases a beautiful woman from his thraldom. The story as told by Soma Deva has already progressed and assumed a form very similar to that of Perseus and Andromeda.

Among the ancient Iranians the same myth prevailed, but was sublimated into a conflict between good and evil. Ahriman represents Ahi, and is the principle of evil ; corrupted into Kharaman, it became the Armenian name for a serpent and the devil. Ahriman entered heaven in the shape of a dragon, was met by Mithra, conquered, and like the old serpent of Apocalyptic vision, "he shall be bound for three thousand years, and burned at the end of the world in melted metals." Aschmogh (Asmodeus) is also the infernal serpent of the books of the Avesta ; he is but another form of Ahriman. This fable rapidly followed in Persia the same process of application to known historical individuals that it pursued in Europe. In the ninth hymn of the Yacna, Zoroaster asks Homa who were the first of mortals to honour him, and Homa replies : "The first of mortals to whom I manifested myself was Vivanghvat, father of Yima, under whom flourished the blessed age which knew not cold of winter, or scorching heat of summer, old age or death, or the hatred produced by the Devas. The second was Athwya, father of Thraetana, the conqueror of the dragon Dahak, with three heads, and three throats, and six eyes, and a thousand strengths." This Thraetana, in the Shahnameh, has become Feridun, who overcomes the great dragon Zohak.

In northern mythology, the serpent is probably the winter cloud, which broods over and keeps from mortals the gold of the sun's light and heat, till in the spring the bright orb overcomes the powers of darkness and tempest, and scatters his gold over the face of the earth. In the ancient sagas of Iceland, the myth has assumed a very peculiar form, which, if it would not have protracted this article to an undue length, I should have been glad to have followed out. The hero descends into a tomb, where he fights a vampire, who has possession of a glorious sword, and much gold and silver. After a desperate struggle, the hero overcomes, and rises with the treasures to the surface of the earth. This, too, represents the sun in the northern realms, descending into the tomb of winter, and there overcoming the power of darkness, from whom he takes the sword of the lightning, and the treasures of fertility, wherewith the earth is blessed on the return of the sun to the skies in summer.

This is probably the ancient form of the Scandinavian myth, and the King of gloom reigning over his gold in the cairn, was only dragonized when the Norse became acquainted with the dragon myths of other nations. In the Saga of Hromund Greipson, the hero is let down by a rope into a barrow, into which he had been digging for six days. He found below the old king Thrain the Viking, with a kettle of quivering red flames suspended from the roof of the vault above him. This king, years before, had gathered all the treasures that he had obtained in a long life of piracy, and had suffered himself to be buried alive with his ill-gotten wealth. Hromund found him seated on a throne in full armour, girded with his sword, crowned, and with his feet resting on three boxes containing silver. We have the same story in the Gretla ; only there the dead king is Karr the old ; Grettir is led to open his cairn by seeing flames dancing on the mound at night. In the struggle underground, Grettir and the vampire stumble over the bones of the old king's horse, and thereby Grettir is able to get the upper hand.

Similar stories occur in the Floamanna Saga, the younger Saga of Olaf the saint, the elder Olaf Saga, the history of Olaf Geirstafaalp, the Holmverja Saga, and the Barda Saga. The last of these is strongly impressed with Christian influence, and gives indications of the transformation of the evil being into a dragon. Gest visited an island off the coast of Helluland (Labrador), where lay buried a grimly demon king Raknar. He took with him a priest with holy water and a crucifix. They had to dig fifty fathoms before they reached the chamber of the dead. Into this Gest descended by a rope, holding a sword in one hand and a taper in the other. He saw below a great dragon-ship, in which sat five hundred men, champions of the old king, who were buried with him. They did not stir, but gazed with blank eyes at the taper flame, and snorted vapour from their nostrils. Gest despoiled the old king of all his gold and armour, and was about to rob him of his sword, when the taper expired. Then, at once, the five hundred rose from the dragon-ship, and the demon king rushed at him ; they grappled and fought. In his need, Gest invoked St. Olaf, who appeared with light streaming from his body, and illumining the interior of the cairn. Before this light the power of the dead men failed, and Gest completed his work in the vault. In the story of Sigurd and Fafnir, the dragon is more than half man ; but in the battle of Gull-Thorir the creature is scaled and winged in the most approved Oriental style.

Let me place in apposition a few of the Aryan myths relating to the strife between the sun and the demon of darkness, or storm.

Indian myth : Indra fights Ahi.

Indra kills Ahi, who is identified with the storm-cloud, and releases from him the pent-up waters for want of which the earth is perishing. Ahi a serpent.

Persian myth : Mithra and Ahriman.

Mithra is clearly identical with the sun, and Ahriman with darkness. Ahriman a dragon.

Greek myth : Apollo and Python : Perseus and the sea-monster.

Apollo identical with the sun, Python the storm-cloud. Apollo delivers his mother from the assault of the dragon.

Perseus delivers Andromeda from the water-born serpent. In other Greek fables it is the earth which is saved from destruction by the victory of the hero.

Teutonic myth : Sigfried and the dragon.

Sigfried conquers the dragon who keeps guard over a hidden treasure ; the hero kills the dragon and brings to light the treasure.

Scandinavian myth : Sigurd and Fafnir.

Like the myth of Sigfried. Other, and perhaps earlier form ; the dragon is a king of Hades who cannot endure light, and who has robbed the earth of its gold. The hero descends to his realm, fights, overcomes him, and despoils him of his treasures.

Christian myth : St. George and the dragon.

St. George delivers a princess from a monster, who is about to devour her. According to another version, the dragon guards the spring of water, and the country is languishing for want of water ; St. George restores to the land the use of the spring by slaying the dragon.

This table might have been considerably extended by including Keltic and Sclavonic fables, but it is sufficiently complete to show that the legend of St. George and the dragon forms part of one of the sacred myths of the Aryan family, and it is impossible not to grasp its signification in the light cast upon it by the Vedic poems.

And when we perceive how popular this venerable myth was in heathen nations of Europe, it is not surprising that it should perpetuate itself under Christianity, and that, when once transferred to a hero of the new creed, it should make that hero one of the most venerated and popular of all the saints in the calendar.

58

APPENDIX 3

Extract from "The Travels of Sir John Mandeville"

And then pass men through the isles of Colcos and of Lango, of the which isles Ypocras was lord of. And some men say, that in the isle of Lango is yet the daughter of Ypocras, in form and likeness of a great dragon, that is a hundred fathom of length, as men say, for I have not seen her. And they of the isles call her Lady of the Land. And she lieth in an old castle, in a cave, and sheweth twice or thrice in the year, and she doth no harm to no man, but if men do her harm. And she was thus changed and transformed, from a fair damosel, into likeness of a dragon, by a goddess that was clept Diana. And men say, that she shall so endure in that form of a dragon, unto (the) time that a knight come, that is so hardy, that dare come to her and kiss her on the mouth ; and then shall she turn again to her own kind, and be a woman again, but after that she shall not live long.

And it is not long sithen, that a knight of Rhodes, that was hardy and doughty in arms, said that he would kiss her. And when he was upon his courser, and went to the castle, and entered into the cave, the dragon lift up her head against him. And when the knight saw her in that form so hideous and so horrible he fled away. And the dragon bare the knight upon a rock, maugre his head ; and from that rock, she cast him into the sea. And so was lost both horse and man.

And also a young man, that wist not of the dragon, went out of a ship, and went through the isle till that he came to the castle, and came into the cave, and went so long, till that he found a chamber ; and there he saw a damosel that combed her head and looked in a mirror ; and she had much treasure about her. And he trowed that she had been a common woman, that dwelled there to receive men to folly. And he abode, till the damosel saw the shadow of him in the mirror. And she turned her toward him, and asked him what he would ? And he said, he would be her leman or paramour. And she asked him, if that he were a knight ? And he said, nay. And then she said, that he might not be her leman ; but she bade him go again unto his fellows, and make him knight, and come again upon the morrow, and she should come out of the cave before him, and then come and kiss her on the mouth and have no dread — for I shall do thee no manner of harm, albeit that thou see me in likeness of a dragon ; for though thou see me hideous and horrible to look on, I do thee to wit that it is made by enchantment ; for without doubt, I am none other than thou seest now, a woman, and therefore dread thee nought. And if thou kiss me, thou shalt have all this treasure, and be my lord, and lord also of all the isle.

And he departed from her and went to his fellows to ship, and let make him knight and came again upon the morrow for to kiss this damosel. And when he saw her come out of the cave in form of a dragon, so hideous and so horrible, he had so great dread, that he fled again to the ship, and she followed him. And when she saw that he turned not again, she began to cry, as a thing that had much sorrow ; and then she turned again into her cave. And anon the knight died. And sithen hitherward might no knight see her, but that he died anon. But when a knight cometh, that is so hardy to kiss her, he shall not die ; but he shall turn the damosel into her right form and kindly shape, and he shall be lord of all the countries and isles abovesaid.

The
EASTERN DRAGON

There be certain beasts called Dracontopides, very great and potent Serpents, whose faces are like to the faces of Virgins, and the residue of their body like to Dragons. It is thought that such a one was the Serpent that deceived Eve, for Beda saith, it had a Virgins countenance, and therefore the woman seeing the likenesse of her own face, was the more easily drawn to believe it : into the which, when the Devil had entred, they say he taught it to cover the body with leaves, and to shew nothing but the head and face. But this fable is not worthy to be refuted, because the Scripture it self doth directly gainsay every part of it. For first of all it is called a Serpent, and if it had been a Dragon, Moses would have said so, and therefore for ordinary punishment, God doth appoint it to creep upon the belly, wherefore it is not likely that it had either wings or feet. Secondly, it was unpossible and unlikely, that any part of the body was covered or concealed from the sight of the woman, seeing she knew it directly to be a Serpent, as afterward she confessed before GOD and her husband.

Edward Topsell,
THE HISTORY OF SERPENTS,
London, 1658.

THE CHINESE DRAGON

We now approach the consideration of a country in which the belief in the existence of the dragon is thoroughly woven into the life of the whole nation. Yet at the same time it has developed into such a medley of mythology and superstition as to materially strengthen our conviction of the reality of the basis upon which the belief has been founded, though it involves us in a mass of intricate perplexities in connection with the determination of its actual period of existence.

There is no country so conservative as China, no nation which can boast of such high antiquity, as a collective people permanently occupying the same regions, and preserving records of their polity, manners and surroundings from the earliest date of their occupation of the territory which still remains the centre of their civilization ; and there is none in which dragon culture has been more persistently maintained down to the present day.

Its mythologies, histories, religions, popular stories, and proverbs, all teem with references to a mysterious being who has a physical nature and spiritual attributes. Gifted with an accepted form, which he has the supernatural power of casting off for the assumption of others, he has the power of influencing the weather, producing droughts or fertilizing rains at pleasure, of raising tempests and allaying them. Volumes could be compiled from the scattered legends which everywhere abound relating to this subject ; but as they are, for the most part, like our medieval legends, echoes of each other, no useful purpose would be served by doing so, and I therefore content myself with drawing, somewhat copiously, from one or two of the chief sources of information.

As, however, Chinese literature is but little known or valued in England, it is desirable that I should devote some space to the consideration of the authority which may be fairly claimed for the several works from which I shall make quotations, bearing on the Chinese testimony of the past existence, and date of existence, of the dragon and other so-called mythical animals.

Incidental comments on natural history form a usual part of every Chinese geographical work, but collective descriptions of animals are rare in the literature of the present, and almost unique in that of the past. We are, therefore, forced to rely on the side-lights occasionally afforded by the older classics, and on one or two works of more than doubtful authenticity which claim, equally with them, to be of high antiquity. The works to which I propose to refer more immediately are the Yih King, the Bamboo Books, the Shu King, the 'Rh Ya, the Shan Hai King, the Păn Ts'ao Kang Muh and the Yuen Kien Léi Han.

As it is well known that all the ancient books, with the exception of those on medicine, divination, and husbandry, were ordered to be destroyed in the year B.C. 212 by the Emperor Tsin Shi Hwang Ti, under the threatened penalty for non-compliance of branding and labour on the walls for four years, and that a persecution of the literati was commenced by him in the succeeding year, which resulted in the burying alive in pits of four hundred and sixty of their number, it may be reasonably objected that the claims to high antiquity which some of the Chinese classics put forth, are, to say the least, doubtful, and, in some instances. highly improbable.

This question has been well considered by Mr. Legge in his valuable translation of the Chinese Classics. He points out that the tyrant died within three years after the burning of the books, and that the Han dynasty was founded only eleven years after that date, in B.C. 201, shortly after which attempts were commenced to recover the ancient literature. He concludes that vigorous efforts to carry out the edict would not be continued longer than the life of its author — that is, not for more than three years — and that the materials from which the classics, as they come down to us, were compiled and edited in the two centuries preceding the Christian era, were genuine remains, going back to a still more remote period.

The "Yih King" or "Yh King".

The Yih King is one of those books specially excepted from the general destruction of the books. References in it to the dragon are not numerous, and will be found as quotations in the extracts from the large encyclopaedia Yuen Kien Léi Han, given hereafter. This work has hitherto been very imperfectly understood even by the Chinese themselves, but the recent researches of M. Terrien de la Couperie lead us to suppose that our translations have been imperfect, from the fact that many symbols have different significations in the present day to those which they had in very ancient times, and that a special dictionary of archaic meanings must be prepared before an accurate translation can be arrived at, a consummation which may shortly be expected from his labours. I find in my notes, taken from the manuscript of a lecture given in 1870 by the Rev. J. Butler, that "the way in which the dragon came to represent the Emperor and the Throne of China (1) is accounted for in the Yih King

64

as follows : " The chief dragon has his abode in the sky, and all clouds and vapours, winds and rains are under his control. He can send rain or withhold it at his pleasure, and hence all vegetable life is dependent on him. So the Emperor, from his exalted throne, watches over the interests of his people, and confers on them those temporal and spiritual blessings, without which they would perish." (2)

The Annals of the Bamboo Books.

These are annals from which a great part of Chinese chronology is derived. Mr. Legge gives the history of their discovery, as related in the history of the Emperor Woo, the first of the sovereigns of Tsin, as follows :

"In the fifth year of his reign, under title of Hëen-ning (= A.D. 279), some lawless parties, in the department of Keih, dug open the grave of King Sëang of Wei (died B.C. 295) and found a number of bamboo tablets, written over, in the small seal character, with more than one hundred thousand words, which were deposited in the imperial library."

Mr. Legge adds, "The Emperor referred them to the principal scholars in the service of the Government, to adjust the tables in order, having first transcribed them in modern characters. Among them were a copy of the Yih King, in two books, agreeing with that generally received, and a book of annals, in twelve or thirteen chapters, beginning with the reign of Hwang-te, and coming down to the sixteenth year of the last emperor of the Chow dynasty, B.C. 298."

"The reader will be conscious of a disposition to reject at once the account of the discovery of the Bamboo Books. He has read so much of the recovery of portions of the Shoo from the walls of houses that he must be tired of this mode of finding lost treasures, and smiles when he is now called on to believe that an old tomb opened and yielded its literary stores long after the human remains that had been laid in it had mingled with the dust. From the death of King Sëang to A.D. 279 were 574 years."

Against this, however, which is not a very weighty objection, if we consider the length of time that Egyptian papyri have been entombed before their restoration to the light, Mr. Legge ranges preponderating evidence in favour of their authenticity, and concludes that "they had, no doubt, been lying for nearly six centuries in the tomb in which they had been first deposited when they were then brought anew to light."

The annals consist of two portions, one forming what is undoubtedly the original text, and consisting of short notices of occurrences, such as, "In his fiftieth year, in the autumn, in the seventh month, on the day Kang shin (fifty-seventh of the cycle) phoenixes, male and female, arrived", etc., etc. It also records earthquakes, obituaries, accessions, and remarkable natural phenomena. The other portion is interspersed between these, in the form of rather diffuse, though not very numerous, notes, which by some are supposed to be a portion of the original text, by others, to have been added by the commentator Shin Yo (A.D. 502-557).

In the latter, frequent references are made to the appearance of phoenixes (the fung wang), ki-lins (unicorns), and dragons.

In the former we find only incidental references to either of these, such as, "XIV. The Emperor K'ung-kea. In his first year (B.C. 1611), when he came to the throne, he dwelt on the west of the Ho. He displaced the chief of Ch'e-wei, and appointed Lew-luy to feed the dragons."

According to the latter, Hwang Ti (B.C. 2697) had a dragon-like countenance ; while the mother of Yaou (B.C. 2356) conceived him by a dragon. The legend is : "After she was grown up, whenever she looked into any of the three Ho, there was a dragon following her. One morning the dragon came with a picture and writing. The substance of the writing was — the Red one has received the favour of Heaven ... The red dragon made K'ing-teo pregnant."

Again, when Yaou had been on the throne seventy years, a dragon-horse appeared bearing a scheme, which he laid on the table and went away.

The Emperor Shun (B.C. 2255) is said to have had a dragon countenance.

It is also said of Yu (the first emperor of the Hia dynasty) that when the fortunes of Hia were about to rise, all vegetation was luxuriant, and green dragons lay in the borders ; and that "on his way to the south, when crossing the Kiang, in the middle of the stream, two yellow dragons took the boat on their backs. The people were all afraid ; but Yu laughed, and said, 'I received my appointment from Heaven, and labour with all my strength to nourish men. To be born is the course of nature ; to die is by Heaven's decree. Why be troubled by the dragons ? ' On this the dragons went away, dragging their tails."

From these extracts it will be seen that the dragon, although universally believed in, was already mythical and legendary, so far as the Chinese were

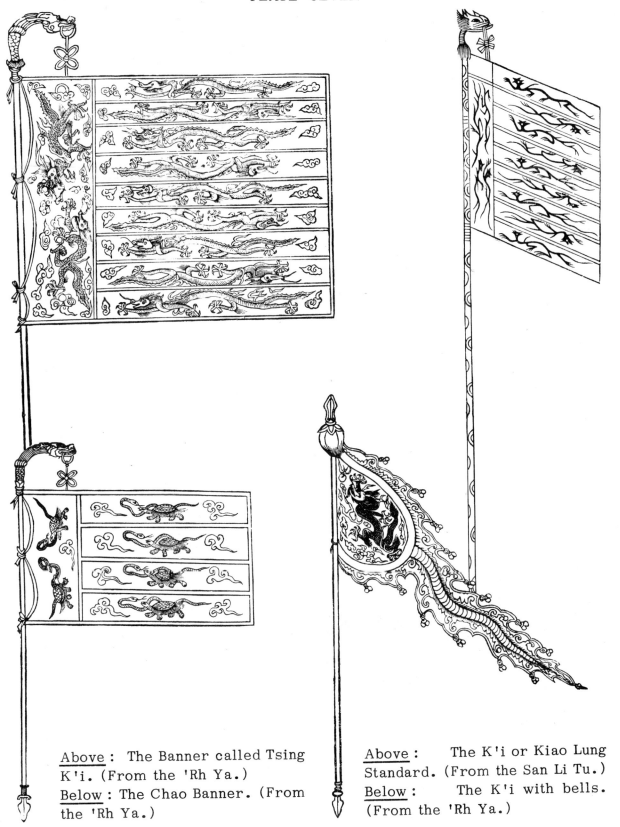

Above : The Banner called Tsing K'i. (From the 'Rh Ya.)
Below : The Chao Banner. (From the 'Rh Ya.)

Above : The K'i or Kiao Lung Standard. (From the San Li Tu.)
Below : The K'i with bells. (From the 'Rh Ya.)

The Emperor K'i, of the Hia Dynasty.

Ping I, a Dragon Spirit attached to the Huang Ho (Yellow River).

concerned.

The "Shu King" or "Shoo King"

The Shu King is, according to Dr. Legge, simply a collection of historic memorials, extending over a space of one thousand seven hundred years, but on no connected method, and with great gaps between them.

It opens with the reign of Yaou (B.C. 2357), and contains interesting details of the polity of those remote ages.

It contains a record of the great inundation occurring during his reign, which Mr. Legge does not identify with the Deluge of Genesis, but which Dr. Gutzlaff and other missionary Sinologues consider to be the same.

It is interesting to find in this work, claiming so high an antiquity, references to an antiquity which had preceded it — a bygone civilization, perhaps — as follows, in the book called Yih and Ts'ih. The emperor (Shun, B.C. 2255 to 2205) says, "I wish to see the emblematic figures of the ancients — the sun, the moon, the stars, the mountain, the dragon, and the flowery fowl, which are depicted on the upper garment ; the temple cup, the aquatic grass, the flames, the grains of rice, the hatchet, and the symbol of distinction, which are embroidered on the lower garment. I wish to see all these displayed with the five colours, so as to form the official robes ; it is yours to adjust them clearly." Here the dragon is chosen as an emblematic figure, in association with eleven others, which are objects of every-day knowledge, and this, I think, establishes a presumption that it itself was not at that date considered an object of doubtful credibility.

Similarly, we find the twelve symbolical animals, representing the twelve branches of the Horary characters (dating from B.C. 2637), to be the rat, the ox, tiger, hare, dragon, serpent, horse, sheep, monkey, cock, dog, boar, where the dragon is the only one about whose existence a question can be raised. From this latter we learn that there was no confusion of meaning then between dragons and serpents ; the distinction of the two creatures was clearly recognized, just as it was many centuries afterwards by Mencius (4th century B.C.), who, in writing of these early periods, says, "In the time of Yaou, the waters, flowing out of their channels, inundated the Middle Kingdom. Snakes and dragons occupied it, and the people had no place where they could settle themselves" ; and again, "Yu dug open their obstructed channels, and conducted them to the sea. He drove away the snakes and dragons (3), and forced them into the grassy marshes."

The " 'Rh Ya "

The 'Rh Ya or Urh Ya, also transliterated Eul Ya and Œl Ya, a dictionary of terms used in the Chinese classics, but more especially of those in the
Shi King, or "Book of Odes", a collection of ancient ballads compiled and
arranged by Confucius.

There is a tradition that it was commenced by the Duke of Chow, 1100
B.C., and completed or enlarged by Tsz Hia, a disciple of Confucius.

Dr. Bretschneider suggests that each heading or phrase in the original
book merely represents the book names and the popular names of the plants
and animals.

The bulk of the work at present extant consists of the commentary by
Kwoh P'oh (about A.D. 300) and, in some editions, of additional commentaries
by other authors.

Notices of the dragon only appear incidentally in the 'Rh Ya as forming
part of the decoration of banners, etc., but these figures of dragons in the
drawings are especially interesting ; as there is fair reason to suppose that
they at least have been reproduced time after time from pre-existing ones
with tolerable accuracy ; and that they give us a good notion of the general
character of the animal they purport to represent.

The "Shan Hai King" or Classic of Mountain and Seas

Short notices of this remarkable work are given by Mr. Alexander
Wylie (4) and Dr. Bretschneider (5), and a more exhaustive one by M. Bazin
(6). It is also largely quoted by Williams in his valuable Chinese dictionary.
Otherwise Sinologues appear to have entirely ignored it.

Mr. Wylie remarks that "it has long been looked upon with distrust ;
but some scholars of great ability have recently investigated its contents, and
come to the conclusion that it is at least as old as the Chow dynasty, and
probably of a date even anterior to that period."

M. Bazin speaks of it as a fabulous description of the world, and
attributes it to Taoist writers in the fourth century of our era, who forged the
authority of the great Yü and Peh Yi. He thinks it would be useless to attempt

the identification of the localities given in it, and offers a translation of a portion of the first chapter in support of his views. The value of his translation is impaired by his making no distinction between the text and the commantary, and he appears to have possessed an inferior and incomplete version.

In an editorial article in the 'North China Herald' of May 9, 1884 (7), it is referred to the date of Ch'in Shih Huang, who connected the Heptarchy into a single kingdom, and conquered Cochin China about B.C. 222.

Kwoh Po'h (A.D. 276-324), who prepared an edition which has descended to us, ascribes a date to it 3,000 years anterior to his time. Liu Hsiu, of the Han dynasty (B.C. 206 to A.D. 25), states that the Emperor Yü, the founder of the Hia dynasty (B.C. 2205), employed Yih and Peh Yi as geographers and natural historians, who produced the "Book of Wonders by Land and Sea". While Yang Sun, of the Ming dynasty (commencing A.D. 1368), states in his after-preface that the Emperor Yü had nine metal vases cast, on which all wonderful or rare animals were engraved, the commoner ones being recorded in the annals of Yü ; and that K'ung Kiah (of the Hia dynasty, B.C. 1879), included this varied information in the present work.

It is to be hoped that at no distant date some competent Sinologue will be induced to furnish a full translation of this remarkable work, with an adequate commentary.

There is no doubt that many would be deterred from doing so by an impression that a collection of fabulous stories, treating of supernatural beings and apparently impossible monsters, is unworthy the consideration of mature intellect, and only fit to be relegated to the domain of Jack the Giant Killer and other childish stories. After a close examination of the book, I apprehend that this view of it can hardly be maintained. That such stories or descriptions are interspersed throughout the work is not to be disputed ; but a large proportion of it consists of apparently authentic geographical records, including, as is customary with all works of a similar nature in China, descriptions of the most remarkable objects of natural history occurring in the different regions. I think it will be found possible to identify many of these at the present day, some may be conjectured at, and the residue are not more numerous in proportion than the similar fables or perverted accounts which figure in the western classic volumes of Ctesias, Aristotle, Pliny, and even much later writers. So far as the supernatural portions are concerned, it must be remembered that, even so late as the days of the childhood of Sir Humphrey Davy, pixies were still supposed by the lower classes to trace the fairy rings in Cornwall ; that quite lately, and perhaps among certain classes to the present day, the existence of the banshee in Ireland, of the kelpie in

Scotland, and of persons gifted with the mysterious and awe-inspiring power of second sight, was religiously believed in. There are few important houses in England whose ancestral walls have not concealed an apparition connected with the destinies of the family, appearing only on fatal or eventful occasions ; and in the days of the sapient James I in England, and among the Pilgrim Fathers in the American States, the existence of wizards and witches was universally accepted as an undeniable fact, proved by hundreds of instances of extorted or voluntary confession, and supplemented by the concurrent testimony of a still greater number of witnesses who genuinely believed themselves to have been the spectators or victims of the supernatural powers of the accused.

An historian of these later times might well have described such things as realities, and we should not be disposed, on account of his having done so, to question the validity of his description of other objects or creatures existing at the period, presuming them to be more consistent with our present notions of possibility.

No one, now-a-days, would discredit the veracity of Marco Polo because he speaks of enormous serpents in Carajan, possessing two feet, each armed with a single claw. That there was a solid foundation for his story is admitted, and commentators are only at variance as to whether the basis was a large species of python, such as still exists in Southern China, or a gigantic alligator, of which he might have seen a mutilated specimen.

It must also be borne in mind that the existence of some gigantic saurian, now extinct, possessing two limbs only, in place of four, is not an impossibility ; as the small lizard, Chirotes, is in that condition, and also the North American genus Siren, belonging to the Newts.

I notice that Retzoch, in his designs to illustrate Schiller's poem "The Fight with the Dragon" makes the monster have only two fore-legs, and this appears to have been a common medieval conception of it. Aldrovandus and Gesner both give figures of biped dragons. There is also a curious drawing in the ' Gentleman's Magazine ' for 1749 — which is transferred into the pages of the ' Encyclopaedia of Philadelphia ', apparently a piracy of an English Cyclopaedia, of what is styled a sea-dragon, four feet long, which stands bolt upright on two legs, and, like Barnum's mermaid, was probably a triumph of art.

Aldrovandus was probably imposed on by some waggish friend, in reference to the biped dragon without wings, two cubits long, which was said to have been killed by a country-man near Bonn in 1572 A.D., and which he first figured and then placed in his museum ; and he evidently fully believed

72

Aldrovandus' Wingless, Bipedal Dragon.

in the Ethiopian winged biped dragon, of which he gives two figures, but without quoting his authority.

Gesner gives a similar figure, after Belon, of the winged dragon of Mount Sinai ; but Athanasius Kircher is more liberal, and gives his dragon not only wings but four legs.

In poetry we find Ashtaroth described as appearing to Faust in the form of a serpent with two little feet.

As to the mysterious powers imputed throughout the <u>Shan Hai King</u> to different creatures, of controlling drought, rain, and fire, or acting, when partaken of, as remedies for sundry ills and ailments, it may be asked whether we ourselves are free from analogous superstitious beliefs ? Will a sailor view without uneasiness the destruction of a Mother Carey's chicken, or a Dutchman, of a stork ? Or is the Chinese pharmacopœia of the present day much more trustworthy as to many of its items ?

As to the human-visaged creatures, both snakes and four-footed beasts, may we not perhaps put them on a par with other fancied resemblances, which hold to the present day, of (for example) the hippopotamus, to a river-horse, of the pipe-fish, known as the hippocampus, to a sea-horse ; of the manatee to a merman, and the like ?

And, lastly, are the composite creatures, partly bird and partly reptilian, occasionally referred to, so entirely incredible ? Is it not barely possible that some of those intervening types which we know from the teaching of Darwin, must have existed : which we know, from the researches of palaeontology have existed ; types intermediate to the Struthionidœ, the most reptilian of birds, and the Chlamydœ, the most avian of reptiles — is it not possible that some of these may have continued their existence down to a late date, and that the tradition of these existing as

The Winged, Bipedal Dragon

the descendants or the analogues of the Archaeopteryx, and the toothed birds of America, may be embalmed in the pages in question? Is it impossible? Do not the Trigonias, the Terebratulas, the Marsupials, and, in part, the vegetation of Australia, form the spare surviving descendants of the forms which characterised the oolitic period on our own shores? Why, then, may not a few cretaceous and early tertiary forms have struggled on, through a happy combination of circumstances, to an aged and late existence in other lands.

After long, repeated, and careful examination of the Shan Hai King, I arrive at a very different conclusion from M. Bazin. I hold it to be an authentic and precious memorial which has been handed down to us from remote antiquity, the value of which has been unrecognised owing to the book being unfortunately a fusion of two and perhaps three distinct works.

The oldest was the Shan King, and consists of five volumes, devoted respectively to the northern, southern, eastern, western, and central mountain ranges. This is devoid of all reference to persons and habited places. It is simply an abstract of the results of a topographical survey which may not impossibly have been, as it claims, the one conducted by Yü.

It contains lists of mountains and rivers, with valuable notes on their mineral productions, fauna and flora. It also gives lists of the divinities controlling or belonging to each mountain range, and the sacrifices suitable to them. There are few extravagances in this portion of the work.

The remainder is devoted to a history of the regions without and within the four hai or seas bounding the empire, and those constituting what is called the Great Desert. Here extravagant stories, myths, accounts of wonderful people, references to states, cities, and tribes are mingled with geographical notices which, from their repetition, show that this portion is itself resolvable into two distinct works of more modern date, whose origin was probably posterior to the wave of Taoist superstition which swept over China in the first six centuries of our era. I must add that the term "within the four seas" does not

The Pa Snake

imply the arrogant belief, as is generally supposed, that this Empire extended to the ocean on every side, the archaic meaning being the very different one of frontier or boundary region ; while the word "desert" has a similar signification.

In that more credible portion of the work which I believe to have been the original Shan King, references to dragons are infrequent. In some instances the kiao (which I interpret as the gavial) is specifically referred to ; in others the word lung is used ; thus, it speaks of dragons and turtles abounding in the Ti river, flowing from one of the northern mountains east of the Ho. From the context, however, an aquatic creature, and probably an alligator, is indicated. From the entire text I gather that the true terrestrial dragon was not an inmate of China, at all events after the period of Yü. I further infer that it was a feared and much respected denizen of the more or less arid highlands, whence the early Chinese either migrated or were driven, and from which point the dragon traditions flowed pretty evenly east and west, beat against the Himalayan chain on the south, and only penetrated India in a later and modified form.

There is a short reference to the Ying Lung or winged dragon ; it is as follows : —

"In the north-east corner of the Great Desert are mountains called Hiung-li and T'u K'iu. The Ying Lung lives at the south extremity.
    (Commentary : The Ying Lung is a dragon with wings.)
"He killed Tsz Yiu and Kwa Fu."
    (Commentary : Tsz Yiu was a soldier.)
"He could not ascend to heaven."
    (Commentary : The Ying Lung dwells beneath the earth.)
"So there is often drought."
    (Commentary : Because no rain was made above.)
"When there is a drought, the form of the Ying dragon is made, and then there is much rain."
    (Commentary : Now the false dragon is for this purpose, to influence (the heaven) ; men are not able to do it.)

The better printed copies of this work are illustrated with a very truculent-looking dragon with outspread wings. A stone delineation of a dragon with wings forms the ornamentation of the bridge at Nincheang Foo. In the interior of China, it was observed by Mr. Cooper, and is given in his ' Travels of a Pioneer of Commerce '. These are the only cases in China in which I have come across illustrations of dragons with genuine wings. As a rule, the dragon appears to be represented as having the power of translating itself without mechanical agency, sailing among the clouds, or rising from the

Yu Ch'iang, the Spirit of the Northern Sea.

sea at pleasure.

The Shan Hai King contains valuable notices of winged snakes and gigantic serpents, as, for example, the so-called singing snakes. Speaking of the Sien mountain (one of the Central Mountains), it says : "Gold and jade abound. It is barren. The Sien river issues and flows north into the I river. On it are many singing snakes. They look like snakes, but have four wings. Their voice is like the beating of stones. When they appear there will be great drought in the city."

The Pa snake, already spoken of, is described as capable of gorging an elephant. The Ta Hien mountains were reputed uninhabitable on account of the presence of gigantic serpents (pythons?), which were said to have been of the colour of mugwort, to have possessed hairs like pig's bristles projecting between the lines of their riband-like markings. Rumour had magnified their length to one hundred fathoms, and they made a noise like the beating of a drum or the striking of a watchman's wooden clapper. The Siong Jan mountains were infested by serpents, also gigantic, but of a different species.

The wood-cuts of Ping I (Icy Exterminator), and the Emperor K'i (B.C. 2197), each in cars, driving two dragons, are interesting in connection with the later fable of Medea and Triptolemus. The two stories were probably derived from a common source : the Chinese version, however, being much the older of the two.

The text as to K'i is : — "K'i of the Hia dynasty danced with Kiutai at the Tayoh common. He drove two dragons. The clouds overhung in three layers. In his left hand he grasped a screen ; in his right hand he held ear ornaments ; at his girdle dangled jade crescents. It is north of Tayun mount ; one author calls it Tai common." The commentator says Kiutai is the name of a horse, and "dance" means to dance in a circle.

Ping I is supposed to dwell in Tsung Ki pool near the fairy region of Kwa-Sun, to have a human face, and to drive two dragons.

The Păn Tsao Kang Mu

Descending to late times, we have the great Chinese Materia Medica, in fifty-two volumes, entitled Păn Tsao Kang Mu, made up of extracts from upwards of eight hundred preceding authors, and including three volumes of illustrations by Li Shechin, of the Ming dynasty (probably born early in the sixteenth century A.D.). It was first printed in the Wăn-leih period (1573 to 1620). I give its article upon the dragon in extenso.

"According to the dictionary of Hü Shăn, the character lung in the antique form of writing represents the shape of the animal. According to the Shang Siao Lun, the dragon is deaf, hence its name of lung (deaf). In Western books the dragon is called nake (naga). Shi-Chăn says that in the 'Rh Ya Yih of Lo-Yuen the dragon is described as the largest of scaled animals (literally, insects). Wang Fu says that the dragon has nine (characteristics) resemblances. Its head is like a camel's, its horns like a deer's, its eyes like a hare's, its ears like a bull's, its neck like a snake's, its belly like an iguanodon's (?), its scales like a carp's, its claws like an eagle's, and its paws like a tiger's. Its scales number eighty-one, being nine by nine, the extreme (odd or) lucky number. Its voice resembles the beating of a gong. On each side of its mouth are whiskers; under its chin is a bright pearl, under its throat the scales are reversed, on the top of its head is the poh shan, which others call the wooden foot-rule. A dragon without a foot-rule cannot ascend the skies. When its breath escapes it forms clouds, sometimes changing into rain, at other times into fire. Luh Tien in the P'i Ya remarks, when dragon-breath meets with damp it becomes bright, when it gets wet it goes on fire. It is extinguished by ordinary fire.

"The dragon comes from an egg, it being desirable to keep it folded up. When the male calls out there is a breeze above, when the female calls out there is a breeze below, in consequence of which there is conception. The Shih Tien states, when the dragons come together they are changed into two small serpents. In the Siao Shwoh it is said that the disposition of the dragon is very fierce, and it is fond of beautiful gems and jade (?). It is extremely fond of swallow's flesh ; it dreads iron, the mong plant, the centipede, the leaves of the Pride of India, and silk dyed of different (five) colours. A man, therefore, who eats swallow's flesh should fear to cross the water. When rain is wanted a swallow should be offered (used) ; when floods are to be restrained, then iron ; to stir up the dragon, the mong plant should be employed ; to sacrifice to Küh Yuen, the leaves of the Pride of India bound with coloured silk should be used and thrown into the river. Physicians who use dragons' bones ought to know the likes and dislikes of dragons as given above."

77

"Dragons' Bones (8) : — In the Pieh luh it is said that these are found
in the watercourses in Tsin (Southern Shansi) and in the earth-holes which
exist along the banks of the streams running in the caves of the T'ai Shan
(Great Hill), Shantung. For seeking dead dragons' graves there is no fixed
time. Hung King says that now they are largely found in Leung-yih (in Shansi ?)
and Pa-chung (in Szchuen). Of all the bones, dragon's spine is the best ; the
brains make the white earth striae, which when applied to the tongue is of
great virtue. The teeth are hard, and of the usual appearance of teeth. The
horns are hard and solid. All the dragons cast off their bodies without really
dying. Han says the dragon bones from Yea-cheu, Ts'ang-cheu and T'ai-yuen
(all in Shansi) are the best. The smaller bones marked with wider lines are
the female dragon's ; the rougher bones with narrower lines are those of the
male dragon ; those which are marked with variegated colours are esteemed
the best. Those that are either yellow or white are of medium value ; the black
are inferior. If any of the bones are impure, or are gathered by women, they
should not be used.

"P'u says dragons' bones of a light white colour possess great virtue.
Kung says the bones found in Tsin (South Shansi) that are hard are not good ;
the variegated ones possess virtue. The light, the yellow, the flesh-coloured,
the white, and the black, are efficacious in curing diseases in the internal
organs having their respective colours, just as the five varieties of the chi
plant (the boletus), the five kinds of limestone, and the five kinds of mineral
oil (literally, fat), which remain still for discussion in this work.

"Su-chung states : ' In the prefecture of Cheu kiün, to the "East of the
River" (Shansi), dragons' bones are still found in large quantities.'

"Li-chao, in the Kwoh-shi-pu, says : ' In the spring floods the fish leap
into the Dragon's Gate, and the number of cast-off bones there is very numerous. These men seek for medicinal purposes. They are of the five colours. This
Dragon's Gate is in Tsin (Shansi), where this work (Kwoh-shi-pu) is published. Are not, then, these so-called dragons' bones the bones of fish ?'

"Again, quoting from Sun Kwang-hien in the Poh-mung Legends : ' In
the time of the five dynasties there was a contest between two dragons ; when
one was slain, a village hero, Kw'an, got both its horns. In the front of the
horns was an object of a bluish colour, marked with confused lines, which no
one knew anything about, as the dragon was completely dead.'

"Tsung Shih says : ' All statements (concerning dragons' bones) dis-
agree ; they are merely speculations, for when a mountain cavern has disclosed
to view a skeleton head, horns and all, who is to know whether they are exuviae

or that the dragon has been killed ? Those who say they are exuviae, or that the dragon is dead, then have the form of the animal, but have never seen it alive. Now, how can one see the thing (as it really is) when it is dead ? Some also say that it is a transformation, but how is it only in its appearance that it cannot be transformed ?'

"Ki, in the present work, says that they are really dead dragons' bones ; for one to say that they are exuviae is a mere speculation.

"Shi Chăn says : 'The present work considers that these are really dead dragons' bones, but To Shi thinks they are exuviae. Su and Kan doubt both these statements. They submit that dragons are divine beings, and resemble the principle of immortality (never-in-themselves-dying principle) ; but there is the statement of the dragon fighting and getting killed ; and, further, in the Tso-chw'en, in which it is stated that there was a certain rearer of dragons who pickled dragons for food (for the imperial table ?).

"The I-ki says : 'In the time of the Emperor Hwo, of the Han dynasty, during a heavy shower a dragon fell in the palace grounds, which the Emperor ordered to be made into soup and given to his Ministers.'

"The Poh-wuh-chi states that a certain Chang Hwa 'got dragon's flesh to dry, for it is said that when seasoning was applied the five colours appeared, etc. These facts prove that the dragon does die, an opinion which is considered correct by (the writers of) the present work'."

The Yuen Kien Lei Han

This is an encyclopaedia in four hundred and fifty books or volumes, completed in 1710. More than eighty pages are devoted to the dragon. These, with all similar publications in China, consist entirely of extracts from old works, many of which have perished, and of which fragments alone remain preserved as above. I give the first chapter of this in the Appendix. There is also a description of the Kiao, of which I give extracts, together with others relating to the same creature, and to the T'o lung, from the Păn Tsao Kang Mu.

THE JAPANESE DRAGON

There is but little additional information as to the dragon to be gained from Japan, the traditions relating to it in that country having been obviously derived from China. In functions and qualities it is always represented as identical with the Chinese dragon. In Japan, however, it is invariably figured as possessing three claws, whereas in China it has four or five, according as it is an ordinary or an imperial emblem. The peasantry are still influenced by a belief in its supernatural powers, or in those of some large or multiple-headed snake, supposed to be a transformation of it, and to be the tenant of deep lakes or of springs issuing from mountains.

I give, as examples of dragon stories, two selected from the narratives of mythical history (1), and one extracted from a native journal of the day.

The first states that "Hi-koho-ho-da-mi no mikoto (a god) went out hunting, and his eldest brother Hono-sa-su-ri no mikoto went out fishing. They were very successful, and proposed to one another to change occupations. They did so.

"Hono-sa-su-ri no mikoto went out to the mountain hunting, but got nothing, therefore he gave back his bow and arrow ; but Hi-koho-ho-da-mi no mikoto lost his hook in the sea ; he therefore tried to return a new one, but his brother would not receive it, and wanted the old one ; and the mikoto was greatly grieved, and, wandering on the shore, met with an old man called Si-wo-tsu-chino-gi, and told him what had happened.

"The latter made a cage called me-na-shi.kogo, enclosed him in it, and sank it to the bottom of the sea. The mikoto proceeded to the temple of the sea-god, who gave him a girl, Toyotama, in marriage. He remained there three years, and recovered the hook which he had lost, as well as receiving two pieces of precious jade called 'ebb' and 'flood'. He then returned. After some years he died. His son, Hi-ko-na-gi-sa-ta-k'e-ouga-ya-fu-ki-aya-dzu no mikoto, succeeded to the crown.

"When his father first proposed to return, his wife told him that she was enciente, and that she would come out to the shore during the rough weather and heavy sea, saying 'I hope you will wait until you have completed a house for my confinement'. After some time Toyotama came there and begged him never to come to her bed when she was sleeping. He, however, crept up and peeped at her. He saw a dragon holding a child in the midst of its coils. It suddenly jumped up and darted into the sea."

The second legend is : "When the So-sa-no-o no mikoto went to the sources of the river Hi-no-ka-mi at Idzumo, he heard lamentations from a house ; he therefore approached it and inquired the cause. He saw an old man and woman clasping a young girl. They told him that in that country there was a very large serpent, which had eight (2) heads and eight tails, and came annually and swallowed one person. 'We have had eight children, and we have already lost seven, and now have only one left, who will be swallowed ; hence our grief.' The mikoto said, 'If you will give that girl to me, I will save her.' The old man and woman were rejoiced. The mikoto changed his form, and assumed that of the young girl. He divided the room into eight partitions, and in each placed one saki tub and waited its approach. The serpent arrived, drank the saki, got intoxicated, and fell asleep.

"Then the mikoto drew his sword and cut the serpent into small pieces. When he was cutting the tail his sword was a little broken ; therefore he split open the tail to find the reason, and found in it a valuable sword, and offered it to the god O-mi-ka-mi, at Taka-maga-hara.

"He called the sword Ama no mourakoumo no tsurogi (3), because there was a cloud up in the heaven where the serpent lies. Finally he married the girl, and built a house at Suga in Idzumo."

The third story runs as follows : —

The White Dragon

"There is a very large pond at the eastern part of Fu-si-mi-shi-ro-yama, at Yama-shiro (near Kioto) ; it is called Ukisima. In the fine weather little waves rise up on account of its size. There are many turtles in it. In the summertime many boys go to the pond to swim, but never go out into the middle or far from the shore. No one is aware how deep the centre of the pond is, and it is said that a white dragon lives in that pond, and can transform itself into a bird, which the people of the district call O-gon-cho, i.e., golden bird, because, when it becomes a bird, it has a yellow plumage. The bird flies once in fifty years, and its voice is like the howling of a wolf. In that year there is famine and pestilence, and many people die. Just one hundred years ago, when this bird flew and uttered its cry, there was a famine and drought and disease, and many people died. Again, at Tempo-go-nen (i.e., in the fifth year of Tempo), fifty years back from the present time, the bird

flew as before, and there was once again disease and famine. Hence the
people in that district were much alarmed, as it is now just fifty years again.
They hoped, however, that the bird would not fly and cry. But at 2 a.m. of the
19th April it is said that it was seen to do so. The people, therefore, were
surprised, and are now worshipping God in order to avert the famine and disease. The old farmers say, in the fine weather the white dragon may occasionally be seen floating on the water, but that if it sees people it sinks down
beneath the surface." (4)

As a pendant to this I now quote a memorial from the 'Pekin Gazette'
of April 3rd, 1884, of which a translation is given in the 'North China Herald'
for May 16th, 1884.

"A Postscript Memorial of P'an Yü requests that an additional title of
rank, and a tablet written by His Majesty's own hand, may be conferred on a
dragon spirit, who has manifested himself and answered the prayers made to
him.

"In the Ang-shan mountains, a hundred li from the town of Kuei-hai,
there are three wells, of which one is on the mountain top, in a spot seldom
visited. It has long been handed down that a dragon inhabits this well. If
pieces of metal are thrown into the well they float, but light things, as silk or
paper, will sink. If the offerings are accepted, fruits come floating up in
exchange. Anything not perfectly pure and clean is rejected and sent whirling
up again. The spirit dwells in the blackest depths of the water, in form like a
strange fish, with golden scales and four paws, red eyes and long body. He
ordinarily remains deep in the water without stirring. But in times of great
drought, if the local authorities purify themselves, and sincerely worship him,
he rises to the top. He is then solemnly conveyed to the city, and prayers for
rain are offered to him, which are immediately answered. His temple is in
the district city, on the To'ang-hái Ling. The provincial and local histories
record that tablets to him have been erected from the times of the Mongol and
the Ming dynasties. During the present dynasty, on several occasions, as, for
instance, in the years 1845 and 1863, he has been carried into the city, and
rain has fallen immediately. Last year a dreadful drought occurred, in which
the ponds and tanks dried up, to the great terror of the people. On the 15th
day of the eighth month, the magistrate conducted the spirit into the city, and,
with the assembled multitude, prayed to him fervently ; thereupon a gentle
rain, falling throughout the country, brought plenty in the place of scarcity,
and gladdened the hearts of all. At about the same time, the people of a
district in the vicinity, called Chin-yu, also had recourse to the spirit, with
equally favourable results. These are well-known events, which have happened
quite recently.

Mural Tablet, from the Temple of Longevity, Canton.

One of the eave tiles from the old Imperial
Palace of Nankin, showing the Five-clawed
or Imperial Dragon, an emblem which
could not be borne by any outside of the
Imperial Service, under penalty of death.
Commoners had to be satisfied with a four
clawed dragon.

Above : The Hai Riyo, a Japanese cross between dragon and bird, from the Chi-on-in Monastery, Kioto. Left and right: Chinese temple medals portraying the dragon in company with the phoenix. Below : An illustration from an antique manuscript of Western China. Further illustrations appear on pp. 99 and 100.

"It is the desire of the people of the district that some mark of distinction should be conferred on the spirit ; and the memorialist finds such a proceeding to be sanctioned both by law and precedent ; he therefore humbly lays the wishes of the people before His Majesty, who, perhaps, will be pleased to confer a title and an autograph tablet as above suggested. The Rescript has already been recorded.

"No. 6 of Memorial."

The idea of the transformation of a sea-monster or dragon into a bird is common both to China and Japan ; for instance, in the 'Works of Chuang-Tsze' we read that —

"In the Northern Sea there was a fish, whose name was kw'en. It is not known how many thousand li this fish was in length. It was afterwards transformed into a bird called p'eng, the size of whose back is uncertain by some thousands of li. Suddenly it would dart upwards with rapid flight, its wings overspreading the sky like clouds. When the waters were agitated (in the sixth moon) the bird moved its abode to the Southern Sea, the Pool of Heaven. In the book called Ts'i Hieh, which treats of strange and marvellous things, it is said that when the p'eng flew south, it first rushed over three thousand li of water, and then mounted to the height of ninety thousand li, riding upon the wind that blows in the sixth moon. The wild horses, i.e., the clouds and dust of heaven, were driven along by the zephyrs. The colour of the sky was blue ; yet, is that the real colour of the sky, or only the appearance produced by infinite, illimitable depths ? For the bird, as it looked downwards, the view was just the same as it is to us when we look upwards."

On the screens decorating the Chi-on-in monastery in Kioto, are depicted several composite creatures, half-dragon, half-bird, which appear to represent the Japanese rendering of the Chinese Ying Lung or winged dragon. They have dragons' heads, plumose wings, and birds' claws, and have been variously designated to me by Japanese as the Hai Riyo, the Tobi Tatsu and the Schachi Hoko.

Mammea the Mother of Alexander Severus the Emperor, the night before his birth, dreamed that she brought forth a little Dragon, so also did Olympia the Mother of Alexander the Great, and Pomponia the Mother of Scipio Africanus. The like prodigy gave Augustus hope that he should be Emperor. For when his Mother Aetia came in the night time unto the Temple of Apollo, and had set down her bed or couch in the Temple among other Matrons, suddenly she fell asleep, and in her sleep she dreamed that a Dragon came to her, and clasped about her body, and so departed without doing her any harm. Afterwards the print of a Dragon remained perpetually upon her belly, so as she never durst any more be seen in any bath.

The Emperor Tiberius Caesar, had a Dragon which he daily fed with his own hands, and nourished like good fortune, at the last it happened that this Dragon was defaced with the biting of Emmets, and the former beauty of his body much obscured : Wherefore the Emperor grew greatly amazed thereat, and demanding a reason thereof of the Wisemen, he was by them admonished to beware the insurrection of the common people.

Edward Topsell,
THE HISTORY OF SERPENTS,
London, 1658.

APPENDIX 1

Justus Doolittle, "Social Life of the Chinese" (Extracts)

Ch. II. p. 264.

The dragon holds a remarkable position in the history and government of China. It also enjoys an ominous eminence in the affections of the Chinese people. It is frequently represented as the great benefactor of mankind. It is the dragon which causes the clouds to form and the rain to fall. The Chinese delight in praising its wonderful properties and powers. It is the venerated symbol of good.

The Emperor appropriates to himself the use of the _true_ dragon, the one which has five claws on each of its four feet. On his dress of state is embroidered a likeness of the dragon. His throne is styled ' the dragon's seat '. His bedstead is ' the dragon's bedstead '. His countenance is ' the dragon's face '. His eyes are ' the dragon's eyes '. His beard is ' the dragon's beard '.

The true dragon, it is affirmed, never renders itself visible to mortal vision wholly at once. If its head is seen, its tail is obscured or hidden. If it exposes its tail to the eyes of man, it is careful to keep its head out of sight. It is always accompanied by or enshrouded in clouds when it becomes visible in any of its parts. Water-spouts are believed by some Chinese to be occasioned by the ascent and descent of the dragon. Fishermen and residents on the border of the ocean are reported to catch occasional glimpses of the dragon ascending from the water and descending to it.

It is represented as having scales, and without ears ; from its forehead two horns project upwards. Its organ of hearing seems to be located in these horns, for it is asserted that it hears through them. It is regarded as the king of fishes.

Proclamations cmanating dircotly from the Emperor, and published on yellow paper, sometimes have the likenesses of two dragons facing each other, and grasping or playing with a pearl, of which the dragon is believed to be very fond.

Ch. II. p. 338.

The sagacious geomancer is also careful to observe the mountain or hill on the right and left sides of the spot for a lucky grave. The left-hand side is called the black dragon ; the right-hand side is called the white tiger. The lucky prospects, in a Chinese sense, on the hills situated to the left, should clearly surpass the prospects of the hills on the right. And the reason for this is manifest, for the black dragon is naturally weaker than the white tiger.

Ch. I. p. 275.

The common belief is that the dragon and the tiger always fight when they meet ; and that when the dragon moves, the clouds will ascend and rain will soon fall.

Hence, in a time of drought, if the bones of a tiger should be let down into this well called the ' dragon's well ', and kept there for three days at the most, there will, it is sagely affirmed, most likely be rain soon.

The tiger's bones are used to stir up or excite the dragon.

APPENDIX 2

Extracts from the "Pǎn Tsaou Kang Mu"

The Kiao-Lung

This animal, according to Shi Chan, belongs to the dragon family. Its eyebrows are crossed, hence its name signifies 'the crossed reptile'. The scaled variety is called the Kiao-Lung, the winged the Ying-Lung. The horned kind are called K'iu, the hornless kind Li. In Indian books it is called Kwan-P'i-Lo.

Shi Chan, quoting from the Kwan Cheu Ki, says : "The Iguanodon (?) is more than twelve feet long ; it resembles a snake, it has four feet, and is broad like a shield. It has a small head and a slender neck, the latter being covered with numerous protuberances. The front of its breast is of a red colour, its back is variegated with green, and its sides as if embroidered. Its tail is composed of fleshy rings ; the larger ones are several. Its eggs are also large. It can induce fish to fly, but if a turtle is present they will not do so.

The Emperor Chao, of the Han, when fishing in the river Wéi, caught a white Iguanodon. It resembled a snake, but was without scales. Its head was composed of soft flesh, and tusks issued from the mouth. The Emperor ordered his ministers to get it preserved. Its flesh is delicious : bones green, flesh red.

The Crocodile

The T'o Fish, we call it the Earth Dragon ... It resembles the dragon, its voice is terrible, and its length is a ch'ang (a hundred and forty-one English inches). When it breathes it forms clouds, which condense into rain. Being a dragon, the term 'fish' should be done away with.

Shi Chan says the T'o character in appearance resembles the head, the belly and the tail. One author says that an animal, which is identified with the crocodile, is found in the lagoons and marshes of the Southern Sea, at no fixed time. Its skin is made into drums. It is very tenacious of life. Before it can be flayed quantities of boiling water have to be poured down its throat. Another author states that the crocodile is of a sleepy disposition, with the eyes (nearly) always shut. It is of immense strength. It frequently dashes it-self against the river bank. Men dig them out of their caves. If a hundred men dig them out, a hundred men will be required to pull them out ; but if one man dig, one man may pull them out ; but the event in either case is very uncertain. Another author states that recently there were found in the lakes and estuaries many animals resembling lizards and pangolins in appearance, which utter dreadful cries during the night, to the great terror of sailors. Shi Chan says crocodiles' dens are very deep, and that bamboo ropes are baited in order to catch him ; after he has swallowed the bait he is gradually pulled out. He flies zigzag, but cannot fly upwards. His roar is like a drum's, and he responds to the striking of the watches of the night, which is called the crocodile drum, or the crocodile watch. The common people, when they hear it, predict rain. The nape of the neck is bright and glistening, more brilliant than those of fish. It lays a large number of eggs, as many as a hundred, which it sometimes eats. The people of the South appreciate the flesh, and use it at marriage festivities. One author states that the crocodile has twelve different varieties of delicious flesh ; but the tail, like serpent's flesh, is very poisonous. The crocodile's flesh cures a host of diseases.

The Jăn Shé, or Southern Snake

Shi Chan says : "This snake is a reptile (having a wriggling motion). Its body is immense, and its motion is wrig-wriggling (jăn-jăn) and slow ; Hence its name, Jăn-Shé. Another author says its scales have hair like moustaches (jăn). It lives in Kwangtung and Kwangsi (literally, South of the Hills). Those that do not lift their head are the true kind ; in this way they were called the 'Concealed Head Snake'."

Sung quotes T'ao Hung King to the effect that its habitat is in Tsin-ngan (Fukien), and also Su Kung, who says that it is found in Kwéicheu and Kwang-cheu, towards the south, at Kaocheu and Houn. At several places in the south of the Hills they are still found. Hung King says the large ones (in their coils ?) are several fathoms in circumference. Those that walk without raising their heads are the genuine ones. Those that conceal their heads are not gen-uine. Its fat and gall can be mixed together. The large ones are more than a foot in diameter and more than twelve feet long. It is a snake, but it is short and bulky. Su Kung remarks that its form resembles a mullet's and its head a crocodile's. Its tail is round and without scales. It is very tenacious of life. The natives cut up its flesh into slices, and esteem it as a great delicacy. Another says : When steeped in vinegar the slices curl round the chopsticks, and cannot be released ; but when the chopsticks are made of grass stems, then it is practicable.

Another says : This snake is a hundred and forty-four feet long ; it often swallows a deer. When the deer is completely digested, then it coils round a tree, when the bones of the deer in the stomach protrude through the interstices of the scales ... If a woman's dress is thrown towards it, it will coil round and will not stir.

Shi Chan, quoting <u>The Wonderful Records</u>, says : "The boa is sixty to seventy feet long, and four to five feet in circumference ; the smaller ones from thirty-six to forty-eight feet long. Their bodies are striped like a piece of embroidery. In spring and summer it frequents the recesses of forests, waiting for the deer, to devour them. When the deer is digested the boa becomes fat. Someone says that it will eat a deer every year."

Another author says : "The boa, when it devours a deer or wild boar, begins with the hind legs. The poisonous breath of the boa comes in contact with the horns ; these fall off. The galls, the smaller they are the better they are." Another says : "Boas abound in Wang Cheu (Kwangsi). The large ones are more than a hundred and forty feet long. They devour deer, reducing the horns and bones to a pulp. The natives use the dolishos and rattans to fill up the entrance to its den. The snake, when it smells them, becomes torpid. They then dig him out. Its flesh is a great delicacy. Its skin may be made into a drum, and for ornamenting swords, and for making musical instruments."

The <u>Yü Hăng Chi</u> says : "Rustic soldiers in Kwangsi, when capturing boas, stick flowers in their heads, which when the snake observes, it cannot move. They then come up to it and cut off its head. They then wait till it exhausts itself by its jumping about and dies. They then take it home and feast on it."

The <u>Shan Hai King</u> says : "The <u>Pa</u> snake can eat an elephant, the bones of which, after three years, are got rid of. Gentlemen that eat of this snake will be proof against consumption." Kwoh P'oh, in his commentary, says the boa of today is identical with the Pa snake.

APPENDIX 3

Extract from the " Yuen Kien Léi Han "

Chapter One : The Dragon

The Shwoh Wăn says : "The dragon is the chief of scaly reptiles ; in the spring he mounts the heavens, in the autumn he frequents the streams. This is favourable." Again, "When the dragon walks he is called sah, when he flies he is a yao."

The Kwang Ya says : "When he has scales he is a Kiao, when he has wings a Ying-Lung, when horns a Kiu-Lung, without horns a Chih-Lung."

The Ming Wuh Kiai of the Odes says the dragon has horns at five hundred years, at one thousand years he is a Ying-Lung.

The P'i Ya Kwang Yao says : "The dragon has eighty-one scales. This is nine times nine, nine is the yang (male principle). The dragon is produced from an egg, in which he is enfolded." Again, it says that the Néi Tien says : "Dragon-fire comes in contact with moisture and there is smoke, with water and it is consumed (i.e., a man may extinguish it with water)."

The Fang Yen says : "Before the dragon has ascended to heaven he is a P'an Lung." The Yih King says : "When his clouds move the rain falls, and the various things put forth their forms at the time he rides upon the six dragons and ascends the heavens." "The first nine : The hidden dragon is inactive. The diagram indicates that the subtile ether is below. The second nine : When the dragon is seen in the fields it is profitable to meet the great man. The diagram indicates that virtue is extended. Fifth nine : The flying dragon appears in the heavens : The diagram indicates the great man creates." Again, "The dragons contend in the wilds, their blood is azure and yellow." Again, "Thunder is a dragon."

The Yuen-Ming-Pao section of the Ch'un ts'iu says : "The dragons begin to speak, yin and yang are commingled"; thence, it is said, the dragon ascends and clouds are multiplied. The Yih King, in all the diagrams, clearly says : "The summer winds arise and the dragon mounts the skies."

In the Yuen-Shăn-K'i of the Hiao King it is said : "Virtue approaches the fountains and the yellow dragon appears. It is the Prince's image."

In the ' Tso-K'i ' of the Hiao King it is said : "The Emperor is filial, the heavenly dragon bears the plans and the earthly tortoise issues a book." The Ho-t'u says : "Yellow gold after one thousand years produces a yellow dragon, azure gold after one thousand years, the azure dragon ; red and white dragon is also thus. Black gold after one thousand years produces the black dragon."

The Twan-ying-t'u says : "The yellow dragon is the chief of the four dragons, the true beauty of the four regions. He can be large or small, obscure or manifest, short or long, alive or dead ; the king cannot drain the pool and catch him. His intelligence and virtue are unfathomable ; moreover he ensures the peaceful air, and sports in the pools." Again, it says : "The yellow dragon does not go in company, and does not live in herds. He certainly waits for the wind and rain, and disports himself in the azure air. He wanders in the wilds beyond the heavens. He goes and comes, fulfilling the decree ; at the proper seasons if there is perfection he comes forth, if not he remains (unseen)."

The <u>Shi Ki</u> says : "The bright moon pearl is concealed in the oyster, the dragon is there."

Books of after the Wei dynasty say, "Persia has three pools." They narrate that a dragon lives in the largest, his wife in the second, and his child in the third. If travellers sacrifice, they can pass ; if they do not sacrifice they encounter many storms of wind and rain.

Lü-lan asserts that Confucius said, "The dragon feeds in the pure (water) and disports in the clear (water)."

Sun-k'ing-tsz says : "The accumulated waters form the streams, the <u>Kiao-Lung</u> is brought forth." Han-Féi-shwoh-nan says : "Now as the dragon is a reptile he can be brought under control and ridden. But below his throat are tremendous scales, projecting a foot. If a man should come in contact with them he would be killed."

Kwan-tsz says : "The dragon's skin has five colours, and he moves like a spirit ; he wishes to be small and he becomes like a silkworm ; great, and he fills all below heaven ; he desires to rise, and he reaches the ether ; he desires to sink, and he enters the deep fountains. The times of his changing are not fixed, his rising and descending are undetermined ; he is called a god (or spirit)."

Hwai-nan-tsz says : "The dragon ascends and the brilliant clouds follow." Again, he says : "This <u>Kiao-Lung</u> is hidden in the streams, and his eggs are opened at the mound. The male cries above and the female cries below, and he changes ; his form and essence are of the most exalted (kind). Man cannot see the dragon when he flies aloft. He ascends, and wind and rain escort him."

The <u>Tihing P'ien</u> says : "Wings beautiful grow for the flying dragon ; hair soft like that of a calf on the <u>ying</u> dragon ; scales only for the <u>Kiao-Lung</u>. Only in pools is found the <u>Sien-Lung</u>." Chang-hang said : "How the <u>Ts'ang-Lung</u> meets the summer and aspires to the clouds, and shakes his scales, accomplishing the season. He passes the winter in the muddy water, and, concealed, he escapes harm." Pan-ku, answering Pin-hi, said : "The <u>Ying-Lung</u> hides in the lakes and pools. Fish and turtle contemn him, and he does not observe it. He can exert his skill and intelligence, and suddenly the clear sky appears. For this reason the <u>Ying-Lung</u>, now crouching in the mud, now flying in the heavens, appears to be divine."

Lun-hang says : "When the dragon is small, all the fish are small ; this is divine."

Pao-pòh-tz says : "There are self-existent dragons and there are worms which are changed into dragons." Again, he says : "Among the hills the Ch'ăn day, called the rain master, is a dragon." Hwai-nan-tsz said : "The Chuh-Lung is north of the goose gate concealed in the Wei-U mountain." The Shan-hai-king says the god of the Chung-shan is called Chuh-Lung. When he opens his eyes it is day, when he shuts his eyes it is night. His body is three thousand li long.

The Shui-king-chu says : " The Yulung considers the autumn days as night. But the dragon descends in the autumn and hibernates in the deep pools ; how then can he say that autumn is night ?" It also says : "There is a divine dragon in the vermilion pools at Kiao-chew. Whenever there was a drought, the village people obstructed the upper tributaries of the pool, and many fish died ; the dragon became enraged at such times, and caused much rain."

The Kwah-ti-t'u says : "At the dragon pool there is a hill with four lofty sides, and within them is a pool seven hundred li square ; a herd of dragons live there, and feed upon the many different kinds of trees. It is beyond Hwui-ki forty-five thousand li." Again, it says : "If you do not ride on a dragon you cannot reach the weak waters (i.e., waters of such specific gravity that even a feather would sink) of the Kwan-lun hill."

The Poh-Wuh-Chi says : "If you soak the dragon's flesh in an acid (and eat it), you can write essays." Again, it says : "The Tiao-sheh is in form like a dragon, but smaller. It likes danger ; hence it is appointed to guard decayed timber." Again, it says : "The dragon lays three eggs. The first is Ki-tiao. He goes ashore and cohabits with the deer or deposits his semen at the water's edge, where it becomes attached to passing boats or floating wood and branches. It appears like a walnut, it is called Tsz-chao flower, and constitutes what is mentioned in the Tao-ch'u as dragon-salt." Again, it says : "Below the dragon-gate every year in the third month of spring, yellow carps, two fish, come from the sea, and all the streams, with speed to the contest. But seventy-one can ascend the dragon-gate in a year ; when the first one ascends the dragon-gate there is wind and rain. It is followed by fire which burns his tail, and then he is a dragon."

The Shih-I-Ki says : "East of the hills of Fang-chang there is a dragon plain where there are dragon skins and bones like a mountain : Spread out they would cover one thousand five hundred acres. To meet him when he sloughs his bones is like the birth of a dragon. Or it is said the dragons constantly wrangle at this place. It is enriched with blood like flowing water."

The Shuh-I-Ki says : "In the P'uning district there are the isles where the dragons are buried. Fu-loo says the dragons shed their bones at these isles, the water now contains many dragon-bones, in these mountains, hills, peaks, and gorges. The dragons make the wind and rain. There are dragons' bones everywhere, whether in the deep or shallow places ; there are many in the ground. Teeth, horns, vertebral columns, feet, it seems as though they are everywhere. The largest measure one hundred feet or exceed one hundred feet. The smallest are two feet or three or four inches. The bones are everywhere.

Constantly when looking for anything they are seen." Again, it says : "It is told of the Kuh mountains in Ki-cheu that when the dragon is a thousand years old, he enters the mountains and casts his bones. Now there is a dragon hill, from the midst of the hill issues the dragon's brains."

The K'ié-Lan Records at Loh-yang say : "You cannot trust the hills in the west. They are too cold. There is snow both winter and summer. In the hills there is a pool where a bad dragon lives ; long ago some merchants rested near the pool, until the dragon became enraged, abused, and killed them. A priest, Pan-T'o, heard of it, and, leaving his seat to the pupils, went to the kingdom of Wuchang to learn the Po-lo-man incantations ; he mastered them in four years, and returned to his seat. He went to the pool and invoked the dragon. The dragon was transformed into a man, repented, and followed the king. The king then removed." Again, it says : "To the west of the kingdom of Wuchang there is a pool in which the dragon prince dwells. There is a monastery on the banks of the pool, in which there are more than fifty priests. Whenever the dragon prince does anything marvellous, the king comes and beseeches him, using gold, precious stones, pearls, and valuables, throwing them into the pool. Afterwards they are cast up and the priests gather them. This monastery relies upon the dragon for food and clothing and the means to assist people. Its name is 'Dragon Prince Monastery'."

The Ts'i-ti records say there is a well in the city of Ch'áng-ping at the brambles ; when the water is disturbed a spiritual dragon comes and goes. So the city is called the dragon city.

The Shi-San-Tsin records say Ho-li has also the name Dragon Gate. Great fish collect below it, in number one thousand. They cannot ascend. If one ascends it is a dragon. Those which do not ascend are fish. Hence it is called the "Pao-sai-lung-man." (Great carp ascend the dragon gate and become dragons ; those which do not ascend prick the forehead and strike the cheek.) Again, it says : "The Lung-sheu mountains are sixty li long ; the head enters the Wei waters, the tail extends to the Fan streams. This head is two hundred feet high ; his tail descends gradually to a height of fifty or sixty feet. It is said that long ago a strange dragon came out from south of the mountains to drink the Wei waters. The road he travelled became mountain. Hence the name."

The Kiao-Cheu-Ki says : "In Kiao-chi at Fung-ki-hien there is a dyke with a dragon gate ; the water is one hundred fathoms deep. Great fish ascend this gate and become dragons. Those which cannot pass, strike the cheek and puncture the forehead, until the blood flows. This water is continually like the Vermilion pool."

The annals of Hwa-yang say : "Only at Wu-ch'ing district does the earth meet the gate of heaven ; the dragon which mounts to heaven and does not reach it, falls dead to this place, hence when excavating you find dragon-bones."

The I-Tung-Chi says : "Twenty li west of Lin-fung-hien is a stone dragon, among the cliffs is a rock like a dragon. In a year of drought wash it, and it rains." Again, it says : "At Yen-T'ang there is a pond called Smoky Pond ; it is north-east of the city ten li. Its depth has never been ascertained. It is reported that long ago a man caught a white eel, and was about to cook it, when an old man said, 'This is the dragon of the river Siang ; I fear calamity will follow.' The man was angry, and, regarding the words as vain, proceeded. The next day the whole village was submerged."

The Kwoh-Shi-Pu says : "At the time of the spring rains the carp springs through the dragon gate and becomes transformed. At the present time, in Fan-cheu of Shansi, there is a cave in the mountains ; in it are many cast bones and horns of dragons. They are collected for medicine, and are of five colours. It is recorded in the Chw'en that north of the Wu-t'ai hills, below the terrace, is Azure Dragon Pool, about one-third of an acre in extent. The Buddhist books say five hundred evil dragons are confined (here). Whenever it is mid-day a thick mist gradually arises. A pure priest and candidates for the priesthood may see it. If a nun or females approach then there is great thunder, lightning, and tempest. If they come near the pool, he certainly will belch forth poisonous breath and they will die at once. Foreigners say that in Piolosz there is a spiritual dragon which goes and comes among the granaries. When a servant comes for rice the dragon vanishes. If the servant comes constantly for rice the dragon does not suffer it. If there is no rice in the granaries, the servant worships the dragon, and the granaries are filled."

Yuin-Chu-Tsih records : "If one sees a dragon's egg in the lake or river there will certainly be a flood."

The Nan-Pu-Sin-Shu says : "The dragon's disposition is ferocious, and he fears bees'-wax, loves jade, and the King-ts'ing delight to eat the flesh of cooked sparrows. For this reason men who eat sparrows do not cross the sea."

The Pah-mung-so-yen says : "The perverse dragon, when rain is wanted, sneaks away into old trees or into the beams of houses. The thunder god pulls him out."

Wu-ch'ăn-tsah-ch'ao says : "There is a great dragon which sloughed his skin on the brink of the Great Lake. Insects come out from his scaly armour. Instantly they are transformed into dragon-flies of a red colour. If men gather them they get fever and ague. If men nowadays see these red dragon-flies they call them dragon-armour, also dragons' grandsons, and are unwilling to hurt them."

Pi-shu-suh-hwa says : "In Suh-chan and Hang-cheu the twentieth day of the fifth month is called the day of the separation of the dragons. Therefore, in the fifth and sixth months, whenever there is thunder, and the clouds crowd together, if they see a tail bent down, and stretching to earth from among the clouds, moving like a serpent, they say, 'The dragon is suspended.' "

Tsu-tz says : "The spiritual dragon leaves the water and dwells in the dry place, and the mole, crickets, and ants annoy him."

Kung Sun Hung replied to Tung Fang Shoh, saying : "Before the dragon has ascended he is of a sort with fish and turtles ; after he has ascended the heavens his scales cannot be seen."

Siu Tsung Yuen answered an inquirer, saying : "The Kiao-Lung ascends to the heavenly fountain. He pervades the six regions (North, South, East, West, Above, Below). He moistens all things. Shrimps and the leech cannot depart one foot from the water."

The Shwoh-Wan says : "The Kiao belongs to the dragon species. When a fish attains three thousand six hundred (years ?) it becomes a Kiao ; on attaining this much the dragon flies away." Again, it says : "(Dragons) without horns are Kiao."

The P'i-Ya says : "The Kiao's bones are green, and they can bring their heads and tails together and constrict anything ; hence they are called Kiao. A popular name for them is 'the horse's lasso'." Another authors says the Kiao's tail has fleshy rings ; they are able to compress any creature, and then tear it with the head.

The Shuh-I-Ki says the eye-brows of a Kiao unite, and their uniting is a proof that it is a Kiao.

The Siang-Shu (Book of Physiognomy) says that when the eye-brows unite the epithet Kiao is applied, because the Kiao Shǎn has crossed eye-brows.

The Yueh-kiu (Divisions of Seasons) says that the season of autumn is unfavourable to the Kiao.

The Kia-Yü (Family Discourses) says that if a stream contains fish, then no Kiao will stay in it.

Hwai-nan-tsze says that no two Kiao will dwell in one pool.

The Shan-Hai-King says that the Kiao is like a dragon and snake, with a small head and fine neck. The neck has white ornamentations on it. The girth (?) is five cubits ; the eggs of the capacity of three catties ; and it can swallow a man.

conclusion

The seed of grasse, commonly called Hay-dust, is prescribed against the biting of Dragons. The Barble being

The seed of grasse, commonly calld

The seed of grasse, commonly called Hay-dust, is prescribed against the biting of Dragons. The Barble being rubbed upon the place where a Scorpion of the earth, a Spider, a Sea or Land-dragon biteth, doth perfectly cure the same. Also the head of a Dog or Dragon which hath bitten any one, being cut off and flayed, and applyed to the wound with a little Euphorbium, is said to cure the wound speedily.

And if Albedisimon be the same that is a Dragon, then according to the opinion of Avicen, the cure of it must be very present, as in the cure of Ulcers. And if Alhatraf and Haudem be of the kinde of Dragons, then after their biting there follow great coldnesse and stupidity ; and the cure thereof must be the same means which is observed in cold poysons. For which cause the wound or place bitten, must be embrewed or washed with luke-warm Vinegar, and emplaistered with the leaves of Bay, annointed with the Oyl of herb-Mary, and the Oyl of Wilde pellitory, or such things as are drawn out of those Oyls, wherein is the vertue of Nettles, or Sea-onions.

But those things which are given unto the patient to drink, must be the juyce of Bay-leaves in Vinegar, or else equall portions of Myrrhe, Pepper, and Rew in Wine, the powder or dust whereof must be the full weight of a golden groat, or as we say a French Crown.

Edward Topsell,
THE HISTORY OF SERPENTS,
London, 1658.

The numerous quotations given in the above pages, or in the Appendix, are merely a selection, and by no means profess to be so extensive as they should be were this work of broader scope. Having a special object in mind, I have foreborne to diverge into those interesting speculations which relate to the dragon's religious significance ; these I leave to those who deal specially with this portion of its history. I therefore pass over the many traditions and legends regarding it contained in the pages of the ' Memoirs of Hiouen-Thsang', of Foĕ Kouĕ Ki, and similar narratives, and omit quoting folk-lore from the pages of Dennys, Eitel and others who have written on the subject. For my purpose it would be profitless to collate legends such as that given in the Apocrypha, in the story of Bel and the Dragon, and reappearing in the pages of El Edrisi as an Arab legend, with Alexander the Great as the hero, and the Canaries as the scene, or to dwell on the Korean and Japanese versions of dragon stories, which are merely borrowed, and corrupted in borrowing, from the Chinese. Nor shall I do more than allude to the fact that dragons are represented in the Brahminical caves at Ellora, and among the sculptures of Angkor Wat in Cambodia.

In conclusion, I must hope that the reader who has had the patience to wade through the medley of extracts which I have selected, and to analyse the suggestive reasoning of the introductory chapters, will agree with me that there is nothing impossible in the ordinary notion of the traditional dragon ; that such being the case, it is more likely to have once had a real existence than to be a mere offspring of fancy ; and that from the accident of direct transmission of delineations of it on robes and standards, we have probably a not very incorrect notion of it in the depicted dragon of the Chinese.

We may infer that it was a long terrestrial lizard, hibernating, and carnivorous, with the power of constricting with its snake-like body and tail ; possibly furnished with wing-like expansions of its integument, after the fashion of <u>Draco volans</u>, and capable of occasional progress on its hind legs alone when excited in attack. It appears to have been protected by armour and projecting spikes, like those found in <u>Moloch horridus</u> and <u>Megalania prisca</u>, and was possibly more nearly allied to this last form than to any other which has yet come to our knowledge. Probably it preferred sandy, open country to forest land ; its habitat was the highlands of Central Asia ; and the time of its disappearance about that of the Biblical Deluge.

Although terrestrial, it probably, in common with most reptiles, enjoyed frequent bathing, and when not so engaged, or basking in the sun, secluded itself under some overhanging bank or cavern.

The idea of its fondness for swallows, and power of attracting them, mentioned in some traditions, may not impossibly have been derived from these birds hawking round and through its open jaws in the pursuit of the flies attracted by the viscid humours of its mouth. We know that at the present day a bird, the trochilus of the ancients, freely enters the open mouth of the crocodile, and rids it of the parasites affecting its teeth and jaws.

NOTES

The Western Dragon

(1)   Propertius, Elegy VIII.

(2)   Aristotle, History of Animals, Book ix., chap. ii.

(3)   Ibid., Book vi., chap. xx.

(4)   Ibid., Book i.

(5)   Ibid., Book ix., chap. vii.

(6)   Pliny, Natural History, Book viii., chap. xxii.

(7)   Ibid., Book xxix., chap. xx.

(8)   "It is probable that the island of Zanig described by Qazvinius, in his geographical work, as the seat of the empire of the Mahraj, is identical with Zaledj. He says that it is a large island on the confines of China towards India, and that among other remarkable features is a mountain called Nacan, on which are serpents of such magnitude as to be able to swallow oxen, buffaloes, and even elephants. Masudi includes Zanig, Kalah and Taprobana among the islands constituting the territory of the Mahraj." — P. Amadée Jaubert, 'Geographie d'Edrisi', Paris, 1836.

(9)   Strabo, The Geography, Book vi., chap. iv.

(10)   Pliny, Natural History, Book viii., chap. xi.

(11)   Ibid., Book viii., chap. xii.

(12)   Ibid., Book viii., chap. xiii.

(13)   Ibid., Book viii., chap. xiv.

(14)   Aristotle, History of Animals, Book viii., chap. xxvii.

(15)   Harris's Voyages, vol. i. p. 360.

(16)   Ibid., vol. i. p. 392.

(17)   Encyclopaedia of Arts and Sciences, first American edition, Philadelphia, 1798.

(18)   See 'Voyage to the East Indies', Francis Leguat, London, 1708. Leguat hardly makes the positive affirmation stated in the text. In describing Batavia he says there is another sort of serpents which are at least fifty feet long.

(19)   Broderip, Leaves from the Note Book of a Naturalist.

(20)   Wallace, Australasia.

(21)   Osborn, Quedah, London, 1857.

(22)   McNair, Perak and the Malays.

(23)   Figuier, Reptiles and Birds.

(24)   Athase Keichere, La Chine Illustre, Amsterdam.

(25)   Vol. i. p. 601.

(26)   Pinkerton, Voyages, vol. xiv.

(27)   Ibid. vol. xiv.

(28) <u>Pinkerton</u>, Voyages, vol. xiv.
(29) <u>Herodotus</u>, The Histories, Book iii., chap. cvii., cviii.
(30) Ibid., Book iii., chap. cviii.
(31) Ibid., Book ii., chap. lxxv.
(32) Ibid., Book i., chap. v.
(33) <u>Josephus</u>, Antiquities of the Jews, Book ii., chap. x.
(34) <u>Pliny</u>, Natural History, Book viii., chap. xxxv.
(35) <u>Lucan</u>, Pharsalia, Book ix.
(36) <u>Herodotus</u>, Book iv. chap. cv.
(37) <u>Diodorus Siculus</u>, Bibliotheca Historica, Book iii. chap. xx.
(38) <u>Strabo</u>, The Geography, Book xv. chap. i.
(39) <u>Virgil</u>, The Aeneid, Book vii. 561.
(40) <u>Lucan</u>, Pharsalia, Book vi. 677.
(41) <u>Ovid</u>, Metamorphoses, Book iii. 35.
(42) <u>Ovid</u>, Fasti, Book iv. 501.
(43) <u>Lucan</u>, Pharsalia, Book ix. 726-32.
(44) <u>Marcellinus</u>, Book xvi. chap. x.
(45) Ibid., Book xv. chap. v. A.D. 355.
(46) <u>Lord Lytton</u>, King Arthur, Book i. Stanza 4.
(47) 'The Harleian Collection of Travels', vol. ii. p. 457. 1745.
(48) <u>Churchill</u>, Collection of Voyages, vol. v. p. 213. London, 1746.
(49) <u>Ulyssis Aldrovandi</u>, Serpentum et Draconum Historiae, 1640.
(50) <u>Cardan</u>, De Natura Rerum, lib. vii., cap. 29.
(51) <u>St. Ambrose</u>, De Moribus Brachmanorum.
(52) <u>AElian</u>, De Natura Animalium, lib. xv. cap. 21.

The Chinese Dragon

(1) In China the dragon is peculiarly the emblem of imperial power, as with us the lion is of the kingly. The Emperor is said to be seated on the dragon throne. A five-clawed dragon is embroidered on the Emperor's court robes. It often surrounds his edicts, and the title-pages of books published by his authority, and dragons are inscribed on his banners. It is drawn stretched out at full length or curled up with two legs pointing forwards and two backwards ; sometimes holding a pearl in one hand, and surrounded by clouds and fire.

(2) "The Yih King (I-Ching) is the oldest of the Chinese books, and is the mysterious classic which requires 'a prolonged attention to make it reveal its secrets' ; it has peculiarities of style, making it the most difficult of all the Chinese classics to present in an intelligible version. "We have multifarious proofs that the writing, first known in China, was already an old one, partially decayed, but also much improved

since its primitive hieroglyphic stage. We have convincing proofs that it had been borrowed, by the early leaders of the Chinese Bak families (Poh Sing) in Western Asia, from an horizontal writing traced from left to right, the pre-cuneiform character, which previously had itself undergone several important modifications."

(3)   I am under the impression that the dragons to which Mencius refers were probably alligators, of which one small species still exists, though rare, in the Yang-tsze-kiang. So also we may regard as alligators the dragons referred to in the annals of the Bamboo Books on the passage of the Kiang by Yü.

(4)   A.Wylie, Notes on Chinese Literature, Shanghai and London, 1867.

(5)   In Journal of N. China Branch R.A.S., 1881. 'Botanicon Sinicum '.

(6)   Journal Asiatique, Extr. No. 17. (1839).

(7)   Presumably by Mr. Balfour, an excellent Sinologue.

(8)   The dragons' bones sold by apothecaries in China consist of the fossilized teeth and bones of a variety of species, generally in a fragmentary condition. The white earth striae, or dragons' brains, here referred to, are probably asbestos. The asbestos sold in Chefoo market, under the name of Lung Ku or dragons' bones, is procured at O-tzu-kung.

The Japanese Dragon

(1)   The first two stories are from the Ko Ku Shi Riyah, a recent history of Japan, from the earliest periods down to the present time, by Matsunai, with a continuation by a later author. The third is given as an ordinary item of news in the journal called the Chin-jei-Nippo, April 30th, 1884.

(2)   The idea of the eight heads probably originated in China ; thus, in the caves in Shantung, near Chi-ning Chou, among carvings of mythological figures and divinities, dating from A.D. 147, we find a tiger's body with eight heads, all human.

(3)   Mourakoumo means 'clouds of clouds' ; ama means 'heaven' ; tsurogi means 'sword'.

(4)   White snakes are occasionally, although rarely, seen in Japan. They are supposed to be messengers from the gods, and are never killed by the people, but always taken and carried to some temple. The white snake is worshipped in Nagasaki at a temple called Miyo-ken, at Nishiyama, which is the northern part of the city of Nagasaki.

For the conclusion of the History of the Dragon, we will take our farewell of him in the recital of his medicinal vertues, which are briefly these that follow.

First, the fat of a Dragon dryed in the Sun, is good against creeping Ulcers : and the same mingled with Honey and Oyl, helpeth the dimnesse of the eyes at the beginning. The head of a Dragon keepeth one from looking asquint : and if it be set up at the gates and dores, it hath been thought in ancient time to be very fortunate to the sincere worshippers of GOD. The eyes being kept till they be stale, and afterwards beat into an Oyl with Honey made into Ointment, keep any one that useth it from the terrour of night-visions and apparitions.

The fat of a Hart in the skin of a Roe, bound with the nerves of a Hart unto the shoulder, was thought to have a vertue to fore-shew the judgement of victories to come. But of all other, there is no folly comparable to the composition which the Magitians draw out of a Dragon to make one invincible, and that is this : They take the head and tail of a Dragon, with the hairs out of the fore-head of a Lyon, and the marrow of a Lyon ; the spume or white mouth of a conquering Horse, bound up in a Harts skin , together with a claw of a Dog, and fastned with the crosse nerves or sinew of a Hart, or of a Roe ; they say that this hath as much power to make one invincible, as hath any medicine or remedy whatsoever.

The fat of Dragons is of such vertue that it driveth away venomous beasts. It is also reported, that by the tongue or gall of a Dragon sod (boiled) in Wine, men are delivered from the spirits of the night, called Incubi and Succubi, or else Night-mares. But above all other parts, the use of their bloud is accounted most notable.

Edward Topsell,
THE HISTORY OF SERPENTS,
London, 1658.